CW01659452

The Dorling Kindersley

ILLUSTRATED FAMILY ENCYCLOPEDIA

VOLUME 15 CONTENTS, UNIVERSE – ZOOS; REFERENCE SECTION

DK

LONDON, NEW YORK, MUNICH,
MELBOURNE AND DELHI

Senior Editor Jayne Parsons

Senior Art Editor Gillian Shaw

Project Editors
Marian Broderick, Gill Cooling,
Maggie Crowley, Hazel Egerton,
Cynthia O'Neill, Veronica Pennycook,
Louise Pritchard, Steve Setford, Jackie Wilson

Project Art Editors
Jane Felstead, Martyn Foote,
Neville Graham, Jamie Hanson,
Christopher Howson, Jill Plank, Floyd Sayers,
Jane Tetzlaff, Ann Thompson

Editors
Rachel Beaugié, Nic Kynaston, Sarah Levete,
Karen O'Brien, Linda Sonntag

Art Editors
Tina Borg, Diane Clouting,
Tory Gordon-Harris

DTP Designers
Andrew O'Brien, Cordelia Springer

Managing Editor Ann Kramer

Managing Art Editor Peter Bailey

Senior DTP Designer Mathew Birch

Picture Research Jo Walton, Kate Duncan, Liz Moore

DK Picture Library Ola Rudowska, Melanie Simmonds

Country pages by PAGE*One*: Bob Gordon, Helen Parker,
Thomas Keenes, Sarah Watson, Chris Clark

Cartographers Peter Winfield, James Anderson

Research Robert Graham, Angela Koo

Editorial Assistants Sarah-Louise Reed, Nichola Roberts

Production Louise Barratt, Charlotte Traill

First published in Great Britain in 1997, 2004
by Dorling Kindersley Limited,
80 Strand, London WC2R 0RL

Copyright © 1997, © 2004 Dorling Kindersley Limited, London
A Penguin company

This edition published in 2004 by MDS BOOKS/MEDIASAT Group in association with MediaFund Limited

www.mediasatgroup.com

All rights reserved. No part of this publication may be reproduced, stored in a
retrieval system, or transmitted by any means, electronic, photocopying, recording,
or otherwise, without the prior permission of the copyright owner.

A CIP catalogue record for this book is available from the British Library

ISBN: 84 9789 537 1 (ISBN of the collection)
ISBN: 84 9789 535 5 (ISBN of this volume)
ISSN: 1744 2214

Not to be sold separately from the Daily Mail

Colour reproduction by Colourscan, Singapore
Printed and bound in the E.U.

UNIVERSE (CONT.)

Scale of the Universe

Earth is tiny compared with other objects in the overall Universe. Distances on Earth are measured in kilometres or miles, but distances in space are so great that these measuring units become unwieldy. Astronomers use astronomical units (au) in the Solar System and light years (ly) outside it.

Earth to the Sun

Earth does not stay a constant distance from the Sun, but moves closer and farther away as it orbits the Sun. The average distance is 149.6 million km (93 million miles), or 1 au. Light from the Sun takes 8.3 light minutes to reach Earth.

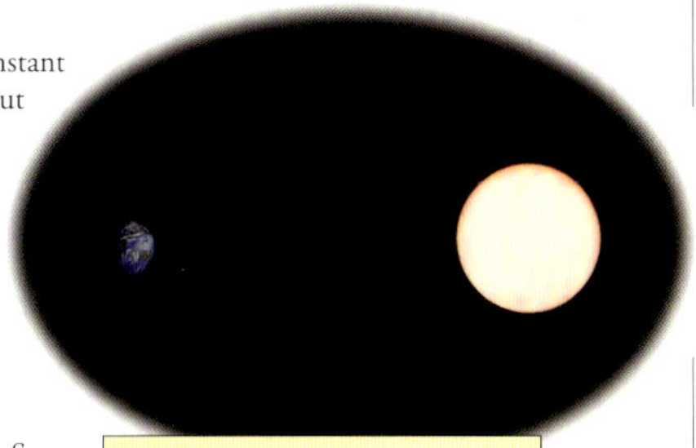

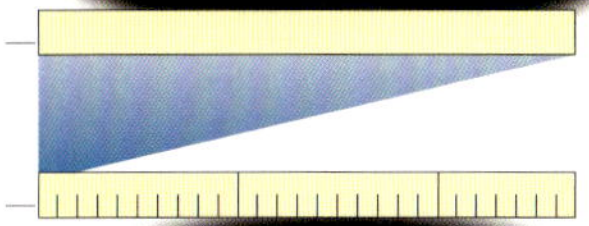

Sun to nearest star

The nearest star to the Sun is Proxima Centauri, 4.2 ly away. A light year is the distance light travels in one year (9.46 million km/5.88 million miles). Less than 10 stars are within 10 ly.

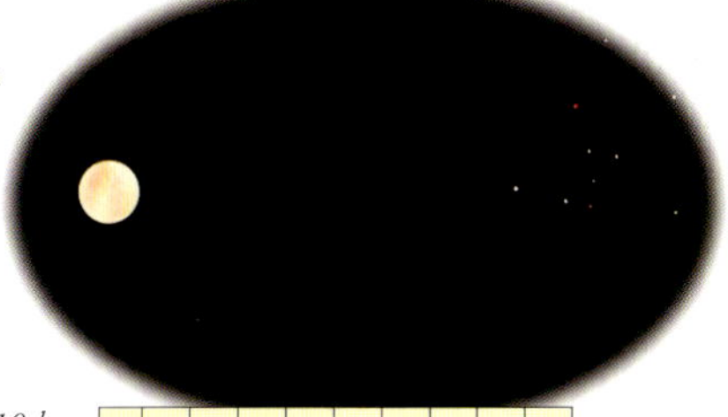

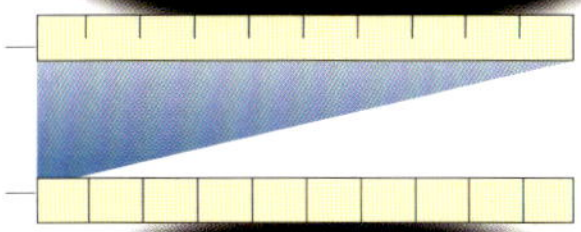

Distance across Galaxy

The Milky Way Galaxy is about 100,000 ly across, and is made up of billions of stars. On average, the stars are 4 ly apart. The Solar System is about 27,700 ly from the centre.

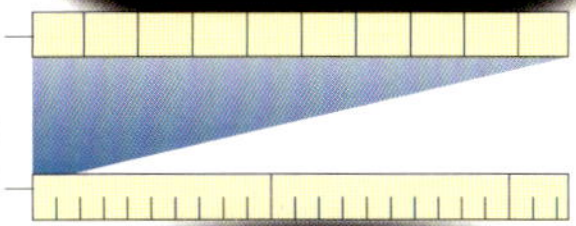

Milky Way to Andromeda Galaxy

The largest of the nearby galaxies is the Andromeda Galaxy at 2.25 million ly away. The Milky Way and Andromeda Galaxy are part of the Local Group cluster, which consists of about 30 galaxies.

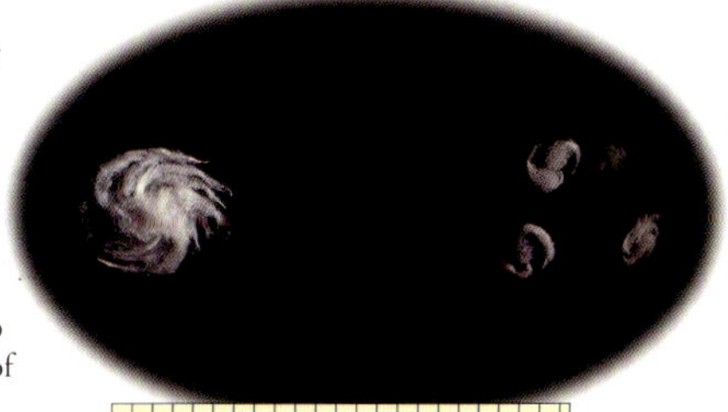

Distance across the Universe

By measuring the distance to the most distant galaxies, astronomers can calculate the size of the Universe. The radius is believed to be 15 billion ly.

Measuring the Universe

The nearest celestial objects to Earth are the Moon and the planets. Their distance is measured by radar. The closest stars, those up to about 1,600 ly away, are measured by parallax. The distance to more remote stars and galaxies is calculated by analysing the object's light or by comparing it with an object of known distance.

Redshift

Light from stars and galaxies travels as a wave, and can tell us if an object is moving away from, or towards, Earth. The light is split to produce a spectrum. If the object is moving away, the wavelength will be stretched towards the red end of the spectrum – a redshift. If the object is moving towards Earth, waves are squashed, and shift towards the blue end of the spectrum.

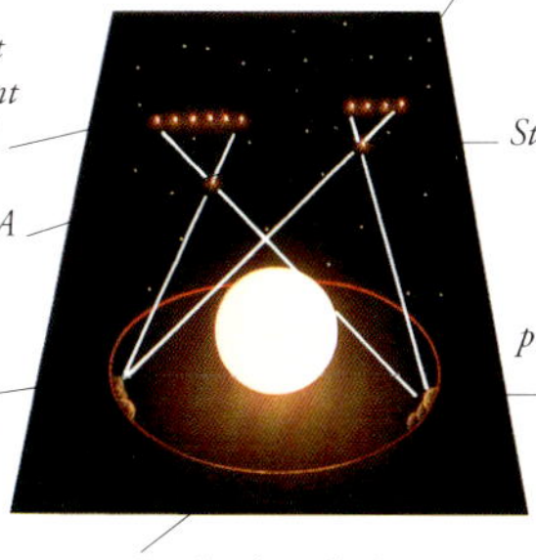

Earth orbits the Sun.

Both galaxies are moving away. But the redder the shift, the faster the galaxy is moving.

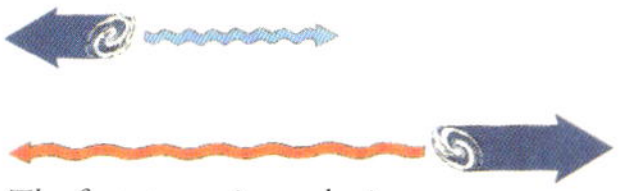

The fastest moving galaxies are the most distant.

Parallax

The parallax method requires a star to be observed twice, six months apart. In this time, the star appears to have shifted against the background of distant stars. The angle of shift – the parallax of the star – indicates the distance. The greater the angle, the nearer the star.

Universe through history

People have always tried to make sense of their surroundings, and different ideas of the Universe evolved as people discovered more. First, they struggled to explain the mechanics of the Solar System. Then, as they discovered more distant objects, the size of the Universe grew. Discoveries of new types of objects brought new questions to be answered.

Babylonian

Gods played an important part in the Babylonian view of the Universe 3,500 years ago. They had placed the Sun, Moon, planets, and stars in heaven and Earth was a large, round, hollow mountain resting on water, and supporting the domed sky.

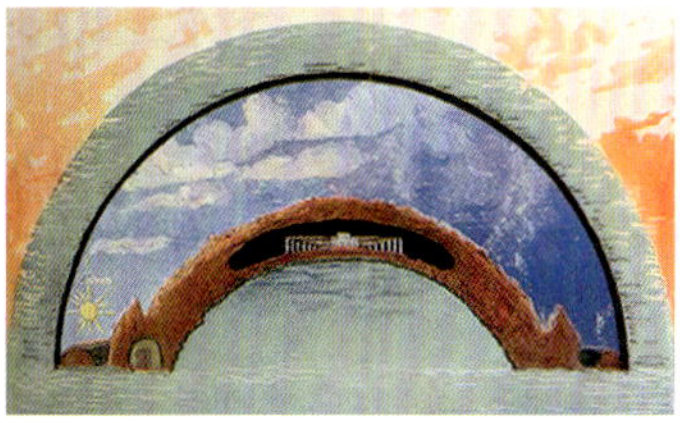

Ptolemaic

The ancient Greeks saw Earth as the centre of the Universe. The Sun, Moon, and the five known planets moved around it. The sphere of fixed stars lay beyond.

Copernican

Devised in the 16th century, this system is the basis of today's understanding of the Universe. Earth rotates on its axis once a day, and orbits the Sun in one year. Earth is no longer at the centre; it is just one of the planets.

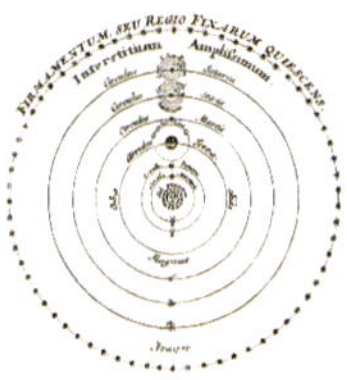

Copernicus

The work of the Polish astronomer Nicolaus Copernicus (1473–1543) marks a change in the understanding of the Universe. He proposed that the Sun, and not the Earth, was at the centre of the Universe. His theories were not generally accepted until the mid-17th century, when astronomers provided the proof that Earth and the other planets orbited the Sun.

Today

Astronomers in the 20th century learnt much about the structure, scale, and history of the Universe. The Milky Way is not the only galaxy: there are millions of them. The Universe is believed to have been created in a giant explosion, the Big Bang, 15 billion years ago. It has been evolving and expanding ever since.

FIND OUT MORE
ASTRONOMY | BIG BANG | BLACK HOLES | GALAXIES | GRAVITY | GREECE, ANCIENT | STARS | TELESCOPES | X-RAYS AND THE ELECTROMAGNETIC SPECTRUM

U

URBAN WILDLIFE

THE MAN-MADE LANDSCAPES of our towns and cities may seem an odd setting for wildlife, but a remarkable variety of animals, from foxes to cockroaches, have made their homes there. Some animals live among the greenery of forgotten corners that re-create wild habitats; others have colonized truly artificial places – even the most sterile concrete structures harbour life. For species such as rats, adaptable enough to try new foods, explore new places for shelter, and tolerate disturbance, the urban environment can be an attractive habitat free of many predators, but full of opportunities.

Types of urban habitat

The typical city offers wildlife an amazing assortment of habitats, from the concrete and tarmac of city centres to the ornamental greenery of parks and suburban gardens. Office blocks harbour insects, monkeys often linger around African market squares, and rubbish tips in North America may be visited by animals as large as polar bears. Railside verges, playing fields, waste ground, and reservoirs alike all have their typical animal residents.

Railway lines
Undisturbed land alongside railways provides a refuge that runs right through the heart of cities for wild plants and wild animals, such as foxes.

Houses and buildings
Many creatures live below floorboards, in attics, and on roofs. Some share our shelter; others raid our food supplies.

Raccoons often tip over dustbins to make their search for food easier.

This raccoon is foraging through the litter in search of food.

Raccoons are found scavenging from dustbins in towns in the USA.

Life underground
Burrowing animals, such as brown rats, live in sewerage systems where they can shelter, devour waste matter, and breed free from disturbance.

Ultimate adapters

Cockroaches colonized Britain after being carried accidentally in imported food from the warmth of the tropics. They now thrive wherever there is artificial heating and food to plunder. They are common in bakeries and restaurants, as well as many houses.

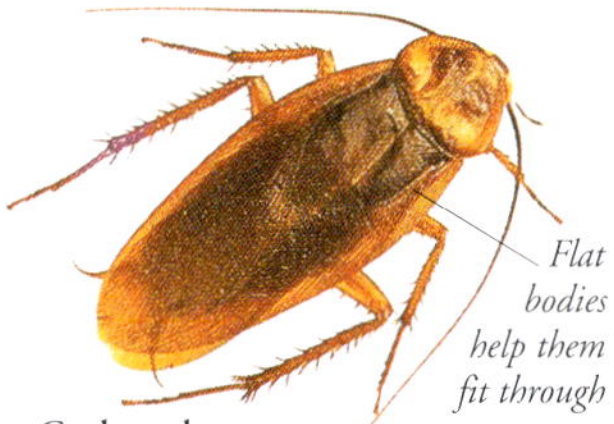

Flat bodies help them fit through narrow gaps.

Cockroach

Source of food

Urban habitats offer rich pickings for scavengers of refuse, waste matter, and the food stored in kitchens, shops, and warehouses. City residents even encourage animals into their gardens by putting spare food out deliberately for pigeons, songbirds, and possums. Gardens, parks, and wastelands also provide plentiful food for non-scavenging animals. Insects feed on the nectar from flowers, birds eat berries, and weasels feed on nestling birds and mice.

Hedgehogs often visit people's gardens where food may be left out for them deliberately.

Re-created habitats

Many of the habitats that exist in urban areas re-create the types of habitat found in the wild. A garden pond, for example, serves as a miniature wetland, while a well-weathered wall resembles a rugged rockface. Buildings are often cliff like on the outside, while their unlit cavities within are similar to caves. It is little wonder that animals used to such habitats have moved in.

House martins used to nest mainly on cliffs and crags under overhanging rocks. Many now build their mud nests below the eaves of houses.

Neatly made mud nest

Frogs and toads have found refuge in garden ponds, as wetland habitats have declined in the countryside.

Many frogs now live in garden ponds.

City warmth
The heating of buildings and the heat generated by machines, motors, and ovens all create extra warmth that has been exploited by urban wildlife. Some birds, such as pigeons and starlings, roost in city centres on winter nights because it is normally a few degrees warmer there than the outskirts. Artificial heating has also enabled tropical insects to colonize buildings in cold climates.

Starlings roosting on ledges of a cathedral

FIND OUT MORE

CITIES | GARDENS | INSECTS | PANDAS AND RACCOONS | RATS AND OTHER RODENTS

URINARY SYSTEM

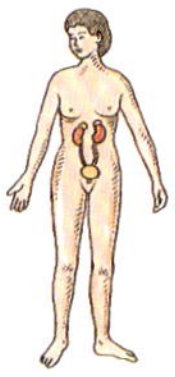

URINATING IS SOMETHING we do daily without really thinking about it. Urine is a waste liquid produced by the urinary system, which consists of the kidneys, ureters, bladder, and urethra. The two kidneys regulate water levels inside your body and filter waste substances from the blood. As blood passes through the kidneys, waste materials are extracted from it to make urine. Two long tubes called the ureters carry the urine to the bladder, and it is then passed out of the body through the urethra.

Kidneys and bladder

The two kidneys are reddish-brown, bean-shaped organs, each about 12.5 cm (5 in) long, attached to the back wall of the abdomen. The ureters gently squeeze urine from the kidneys to the bladder where it is stored. The bladder opens to the outside of the body through the urethra.

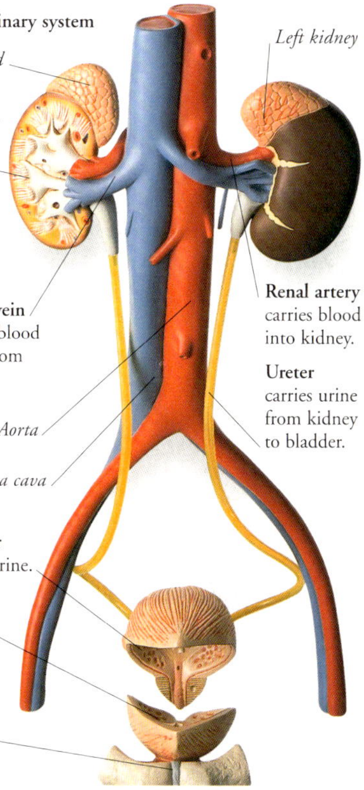

Female urinary system

Renal vein carries blood away from kidney.

Renal artery carries blood into kidney.

Ureter carries urine from kidney to bladder.

Bladder stores urine.

Urethra carries urine to outside of body.

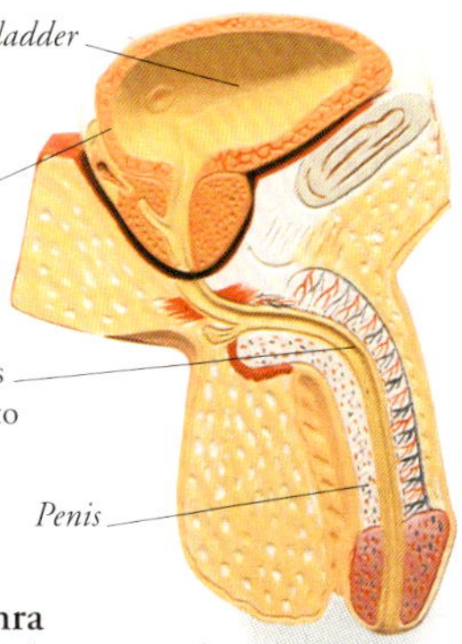

Male urinary system

Urethra runs along penis to outside the body.

Male urethra

The urethra is longer in males than in females. The male urethra passes along the middle of the penis. It has two roles in the male body: it carries urine from the bladder during urination; and plays a part in sexual reproduction when sperm travel along the urethra during ejaculation.

How the kidney works

Each kidney is divided into an outer cortex and a middle medulla where urine is produced. Each cortex and medulla contain about one million tiny filtration units called nephrons. Nephrons filter fluid from blood as it passes through the kidney, and then process it. Useful substances pass back into the bloodstream and unwanted substances form urine.

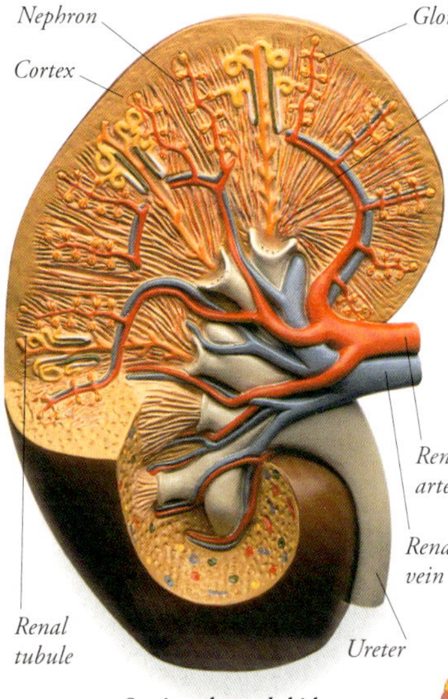

Section through kidney

Nephrons

Each nephron consists of a long tubule with a cup-shaped structure called Bowman's capsule at one end. Fluid passes into Bowman's capsule and travels along the tubule, where useful substances such as glucose are reabsorbed.

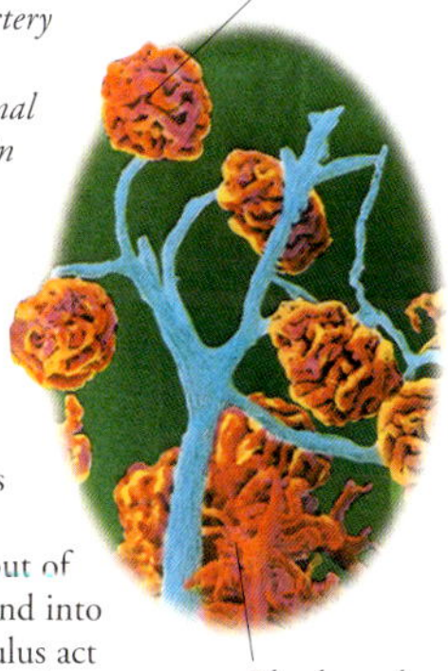

Glomeruli

Each glomerulus (plural: glomeruli) consists of a knot of blood vessels within Bowman's capsule. High blood pressure forces liquid out of the blood passing through the glomerulus and into Bowman's capsule. The walls of the glomerulus act as a filter. Water, salts, and other small molecules can pass into the tubules of the nephron, while blood cells cannot.

Carl Ludwig

The German physiologist Carl Ludwig (1816–95) fully explained the workings of the kidney. He determined that, once inside the kidney, blood was filtered through the glomeruli into Bowman's capsule before being concentrated in the long tubules of the nephron to form urine, which was then expelled from the body.

Bladder

Urine is produced continuously by the kidneys. The bladder stores urine until it is convenient to release it. At the base of the bladder, guarding the exit to the urethra, there are two rings of muscles called sphincters. As the bladder fills, the sphincters contract to prevent any leakage.

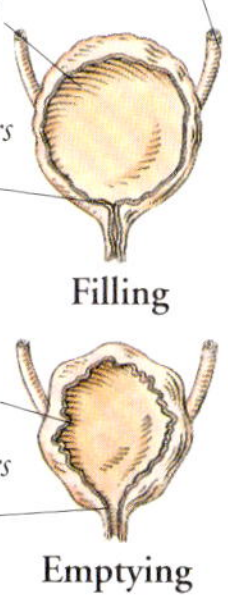

Controlling bladder

You can decide when you want to urinate. One of the sphincter muscles only relaxes when you tell it to. We learn to control our bladders in childhood.

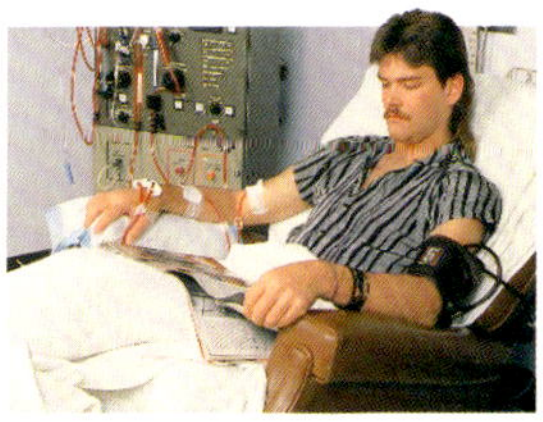

Renal dialysis

If someone's kidneys stop working properly, poisonous waste products can build up in the blood making that person very ill. Kidney failure can be treated by renal dialysis; this uses an artificial kidney or kidney machine to "clean" the blood.

Water balance

Over half of your body is water. In order to work properly, your body must keep its water content at a constant level. However, water is constantly being lost from the body as urine and in other ways (see right). To balance these daily losses, we must take in more water by drinking regularly.

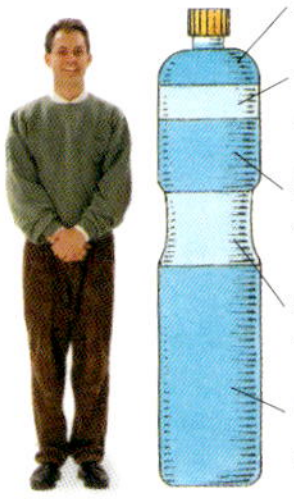

FIND OUT MORE
DIGESTION · HUMAN BODY · LIQUIDS · MEDICINE · MUSCLES AND MOVEMENT

V

VESALIUS, ANDREAS

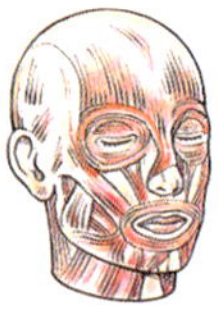

DURING THE 16TH CENTURY, physicians followed the methods laid down by ancient Greek doctors more than 1,500 years before. One Flemish doctor, Andreas Vesalius, challenged these teachings. He dissected human corpses to discover how the body worked, and then published his findings in a book, giving physicians the first reliable guide to human anatomy. By basing his conclusions only on research, Vesalius set new standards for medicine that have survived until today.

Early life
Andreas Vesalius was born in 1514 in the Flemish city of Brussels. His father was a pharmacist and encouraged his son to study medicine. Andreas began his studies in Paris. Vesalius learned about anatomy from the books of the Greek writer Galen. He later moved to Louvain near Brussels and then to Padua, Italy, where he took his medical degree at the university in 1537. The authorities at Padua recognized his talent and made him a professor of anatomy.

Early work

Vesalius was fascinated by anatomy, but was frustrated at the primitive knowledge of most anatomists. In the 16th century, it was almost unheard of for a doctor to dissect a human corpse to find out how the body worked. Vesalius wanted to do this, but he knew he would face opposition from the Roman Catholic Church, whose priests thought that cutting up a dead body was wrong.

Galen
Galen of Pergamum (129–199) was a Greek medical scientist. He experimented on animals, such as pigs and apes, to find out about their anatomy. Galen and his followers assumed that the inner organs of humans were similar to those of pigs and apes. Galen also established the importance of diagnosis and observation in treating disease.

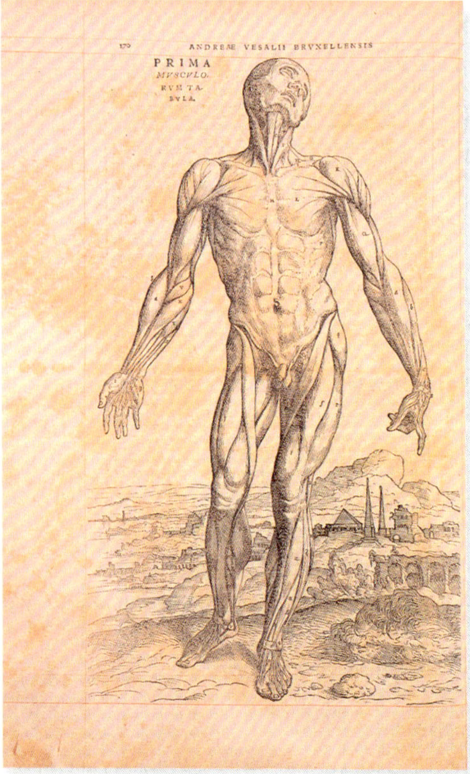

Structure of the human body
In 1543, Vesalius published *De Humani Corporis Fabrica (On the Structure of the Human Body)*. The book contained many woodcut illustrations by the German artist John Stephen, depicting the results of the dissections that Vesalius had carried out. Vesalius challenged many earlier teachings, recognizing that Galen's beliefs rested on a knowledge of animals rather than humans. For the first time, an accurate guide to the human body was available.

Dissection

In spite of the objections of other doctors backed by the Church, Vesalius continued dissecting corpses. As he worked, he made careful drawings of the different functional systems of the body – such as the blood vessels, muscles, and digestive system. These detailed, first-hand studies put him in the forefront of medical science.

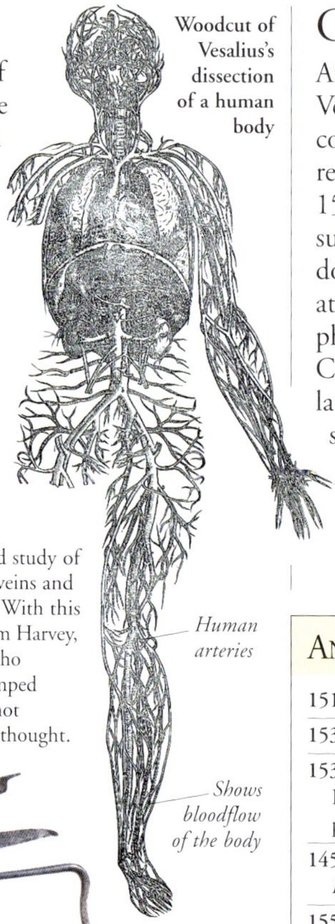

Woodcut of Vesalius's dissection of a human body

Human arteries

Shows bloodflow of the body

Arteries
In his book, Vesalius made a detailed study of the blood vessels, showing how the veins and arteries linked together in the body. With this work, he prepared the way for William Harvey, the 17th-century English scientist who correctly proposed that blood is pumped around the body by the heart, and not produced by the liver, as Galen had thought.

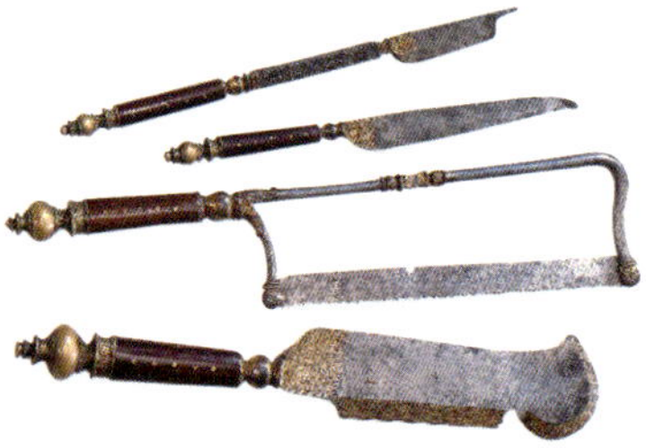

Vesalius's dissecting tools

Controversy

After his book was published, Vesalius continued to dissect corpses, and he published a revised version of the work in 1555. But his work attracted such controversy from other doctors that he resigned his post at Padua and became personal physician to the emperor Charles V and later to Charles's son Philip II of Spain.

Holy Roman Emperor Charles V

ANDREAS VESALIUS

1514 Born in Brussels.

1530s Studies in Paris and Louvain.

1537 Gains his medical degree from Padua University, where he becomes a professor.

1453 Publishes *De Humani Corporis Fabrica.*

1550s Works as physician to Charles V and then Philip II of Spain.

1555 Publishes revised edition of *Fabrica.*

1563 Goes on pilgrimage to Jerusalem.

1564 Dies in Greece on his way back from Jerusalem.

FIND OUT MORE
HEART AND CIRCULATORY SYSTEM
MEDICINE, HISTORY OF
SCIENCE, HISTORY OF

VIDEO

ALL THE EXCITEMENT of a sports event or the happy memories of a birthday party can be captured using video. Video is the recording and playing back of television (TV) signals. A television signal is an electric current or digital transmission produced by a television camera. The signal carries both picture (video) and sound (audio) information that can be used to recreate a moving scene on a TV screen or computer. Video cassette recorders can record TV signals on to magnetic tape, and then play them back on a television screen. Nowadays, much video technology is digital.

Video cassette recorder with top removed

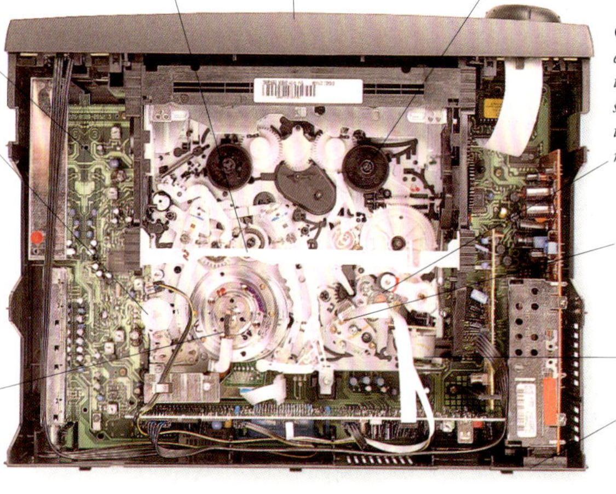

Video cassette recorder (VCR)

A video cassette contains a reel of magnetic tape that stores a TV signal as changing patterns of magnetism. Inside a VCR, the tape moves past a video-head drum, which converts the patterns back into a video signal. The audio signal is picked up by a separate audio head. The signals are then sent to a TV set, which recreates the sounds and pictures. The audio and video heads can also record signals fed into the VCR via an aerial.

Diagonal scanning

The VCR records the information in the video signal as a series of diagonal tracks across the magnetic tape. To read the tracks, the video-head drum is set at an angle, so that it scans the tape diagonally. The audio information is recorded along the edge of the tape.

Camcorder

A camcorder is a combined video camera and recorder in a hand-held unit. Until recently, most camcorders were analogue, which means that the image signal is captured electrically on tape. Today, digital camcorders are more popular because they have the advantage of producing a high-quality image that can be replayed over time without deteriorating. The digital image signal is recorded on tape using a binary computer code.

Digital camcorder

Digital video types

The two types of digital video format are Digital8 and the smaller MiniDV. Both produce crystal-clear images that can be edited easily on a home computer.

Using a camcorder

A camcorder is very simple to use: just point it at the scene you want to capture and press the "record" button. You can zoom in for a close-up or zoom out for a wider view, and use the controls to get the best lighting conditions. A playback screen allows you to view what you have recorded.

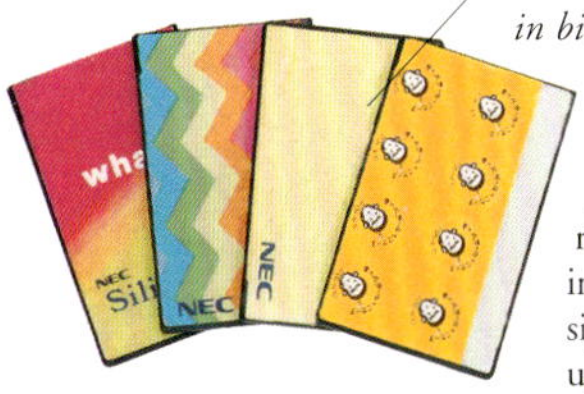

Digital memory cards

Digital memory card

Some analogue camcorders can be partially upgraded to digital quality by recording the signal on to a plastic card instead of a tape. The card stores the signal digitally, as binary numbers made up of the digits 0 and 1. This produces better quality sound and pictures overall.

Uses of video

Video recording brings us news from around the world in an instant. The VCR makes it possible to record TV shows when we are doing something else, and watch films at home after release at theatres. Video cameras in shops and banks also help deter criminals.

Home entertainment

Most towns have shops where people can rent or buy video cassettes or digital video discs (DVDs). DVDs have superb image quality that does not fade.

Broadcasting

All the different elements of a TV show are pieced together and recorded on to video tape. The tape is then played back to viewers over the TV network.

Security

Shops, banks, and many other buildings install video cameras to catch thieves. The pictures the cameras produce can be used in court to help identify criminals.

News gathering

Reporters send video pictures of world events back to TV stations by cable or by radio waves, bringing news to the viewers almost as it happens.

FIND OUT MORE: CAMERAS | ELECTRONICS | FILMS AND FILM-MAKING | LIGHT | PHOTOGRAPHY | SOUND RECORDING | TELEPHONES | TELEVISION

VIETNAM, CAMBODIA, AND LAOS

THE COUNTRIES OF VIETNAM, Cambodia, and Laos form the eastern half of the Southeast Asian peninsula and for many years were known as Indochina. People from China migrated there about 2,000 years ago. The French colonized the area during the 1800s as French Indochina. Japan occupied Indochina in World War II (1939–45), and urged the people to seek independence. The French resisted this move, but were defeated in a war that raged from 1946 to 1954, when all three countries gained their independence.

Physical features

The region is a mixture of rugged, forested uplands and fertile river valleys. The only large lake is the Tonlé Sap in Cambodia. For seven months of the year it feeds the Mekong River, but in the monsoon the Mekong feeds water into the lake, making it ten times larger.

Ha Long Bay
A legend says that the fantastic limestone rocks and thousands of islands and caves of Ha Long Bay on Vietnam's Red River Delta were formed when a dragon smashed up the coast.

Mekong River
The world's tenth longest river, the Mekong rises in Tibet and flows for 4,180 km (2,600 miles) through China, Burma, Laos, and Cambodia, ending in a vast delta in south Vietnam. Many people live in riverside towns and villages and use the water to cultivate rice and other crops.

Forests
Dense rainforest covers much of the region, particularly the upland areas. These forests are home to scattered groups of hill peoples who clear small areas for farming. Hardwoods, such as teak and rosewood, are a significant resource in both Cambodia and Laos.

Regional climate
Cambodia, Laos, and southern Vietnam have a tropical climate with high temperatures all year round. The dry season ends in May with the arrival of the monsoon rains, which last until October. Northern Vietnam and Laos have cooler, more humid winters.

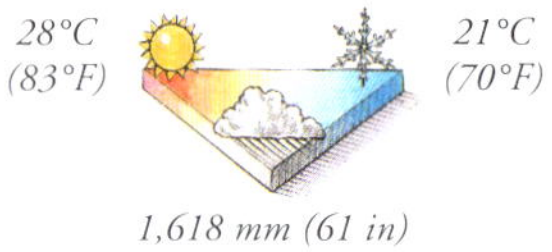

Rice

Rice is the staple food of Southeast Asia, where the warm, humid weather and plentiful water make it easy to grow. Vietnam is the world's fifth largest producer of rice, and one of the largest exporters. The most important growing areas lie in the deltas of the Mekong and Red rivers.

Rice picker, Phnom Penh, Cambodia

Vietnam

For 18 years, Vietnam was torn by a vicious war between the communist north and US-backed south, which devastated the economy. In 1975, the north won the war, and the country was unified. Today, Vietnam is slowly re-establishing its industrial strength and has close trade links with Japan, Eastern Europe, and Southeast Asia.

Boat people
After the end of the war, about a million Vietnamese set sail for Hong Kong, Singapore, and Malaysia, hoping to find refuge in the West. Crowded into tiny boats in appalling conditions, thousands died on the journey. Most were sent home, but some still live in Hong Kong.

Transport
Few Vietnamese can afford cars, and people rely on scooters, motorbikes and, more commonly, bicycles for travelling to work, to school, or to the shops. Rush hour is dominated by thousands of cyclists ringing their bells and shouting warnings. Heavy freight is transported mostly on the rivers.

Vietnam Facts

Capital city	Hanoi
Area	329,560 sq km (127,243 sq miles)
Population	79,200,000
Main language	Vietnamese
Major religions	Buddhist, Christian
Currency	Dông

Fishing
Seafood and fish are an important part of Vietnamese cooking. Thousands of people earn their living by fishing off the long coastline and in the river deltas. They catch more than a million tonnes of lobsters, fish, squid, and shrimps every year.

Cambodia

Once at the centre of the Khmer Empire, Cambodia was ravaged by war during the 20th century. From 1975 to 1979, the country was terrorized by the communist Khmer Rouge led by Pol Pot. More than a million people were killed, many of whom were intellectuals. Today, a democratic government is slowly rebuilding the shattered economy.

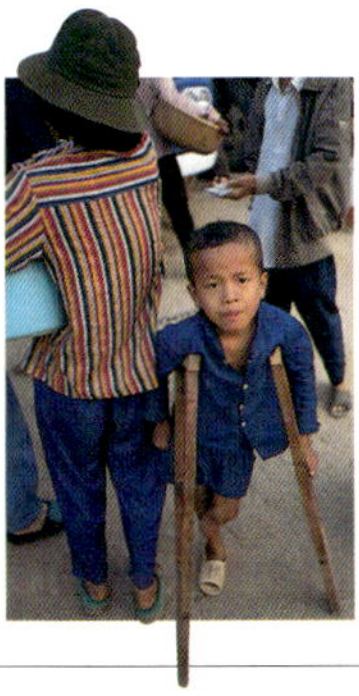

Minefields
More than three million active mines were left in the ground after the wars in Cambodia. As a result, thousands of people have been maimed or disabled.

Classical dance
The highly stylized classical dance of Cambodia is based on religious dances originally performed in the 12th-century temple complex of Angkor Wat. The dancers spend years perfecting the graceful movements, and wear costumes that are so tight they must be sewn on before each performance.

Khmers
Around 90 per cent of Cambodians are Khmers, an ancient people who had a flourishing kingdom two thousand years ago. Most live in small rural villages, where houses are often built on stilts to avoid flooding during the monsoon rains.

Cambodia Facts

Capital city	Phnom Penh
Area	181,040 sq km (69,900 sq miles)
Population	13,400,000
Main languages	Khmer, Chinese, Vietnamese
Major religion	Buddhist
Currency	Riel

Laos

Surrounded by land on all sides, Laos has rich reserves of tin, lead, and zinc as well as iron, coal, and timber, yet it remains one of the world's least developed nations. About 80 per cent of the people work on the land, growing just enough food for themselves. Since 1975, Laos has been under communist rule.

Buddhism
More than half of the people in Laos are Theravada Buddhists, a branch of Buddhism that originated in Sri Lanka. Theravada means the "way of the Elders" and encourages followers to reduce suffering in the world.

Friendship Bridge
The Mekong River forms a natural border between Laos and neighbouring Thailand. Since 1988, there has been increased trade between the two countries, and in 1994, with Australian finance, a "Friendship Bridge" was built over the river's lower reaches. It connects Vientiane with the Thai town of Nong Khai, and gives Laos access to Thai ports.

Laos Facts

Capital city	Vientiane
Area	236,800 sq km (91,428 sq miles)
Population	5,400,000
Main languages	Lao, Miao, Yao
Major religions	Buddhist, traditional beliefs
Currency	Laotian New Kip

Hill tribeswoman

Kha peoples
The Kha, the many hill peoples of Laos, were the country's first inhabitants. For centuries the Lao have treated them like slaves. The Kha live in scattered villages, and speak many different languages. They use traditional slash-and-burn farming methods to grow crops, and opium poppies for the drugs trade.

FIND OUT MORE
Asia | Asia, history of | Bridges | Buddhism | Dance | Empires | Farming | Governments and politics | Khmer Empire | United States, history of

VIKINGS

FROM THE 8TH to the 11th centuries, the powerful Vikings emerged from their homelands in Norway, Sweden, and Denmark, and swept across Europe. They were superb ship-builders and navigators, and they used these skills to travel as far afield as the eastern coast of North America, and the eastern Mediterranean. Vikings had a reputation for raiding wherever they landed, and many of their leaders grew wealthy from plunder. However, they were not all raiders – some established peaceful colonies.

Exploration

Travelling by sea from Scandinavia, the Vikings raided and settled along the coasts of Europe, and crossed the Atlantic to Iceland, Greenland, and Newfoundland. They also sailed the rivers of Europe to Russia and Constantinople.

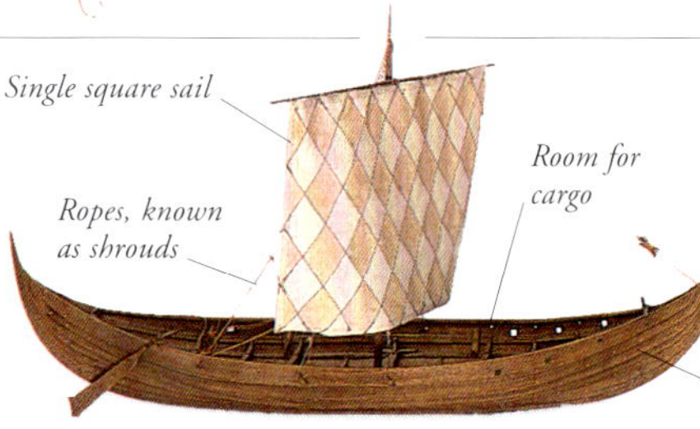

A knarr, or full-bellied ship, took settlers to Greenland.

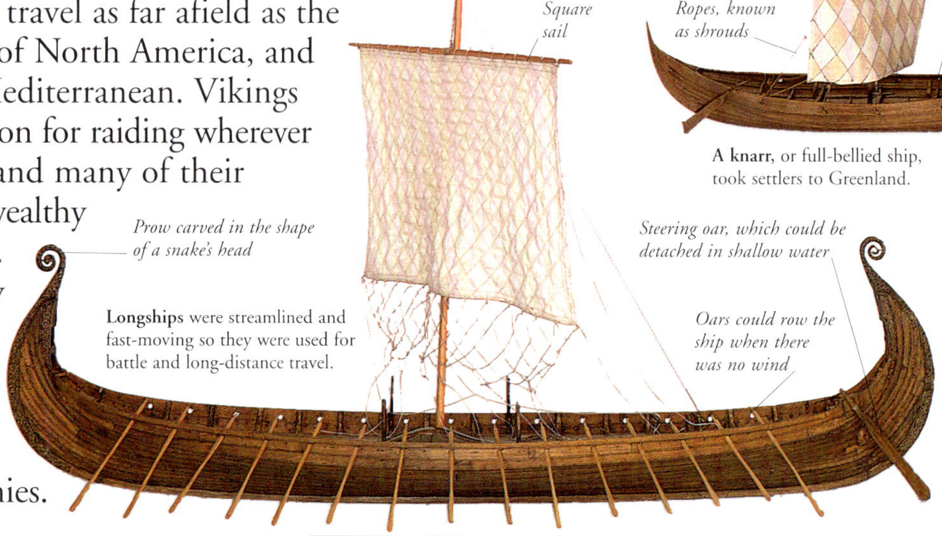

Longships were streamlined and fast-moving so they were used for battle and long-distance travel.

Ships

All Viking ships had a keel, matching prow and stern, and were built with overlapping planks. Long, fast ships were used for raiding trips, while fatter vessels, with a large capacity, were used for carrying cargo.

Raiders

In 793 a group of Vikings raided the monastery of Lindisfarne, northern England. The attack was the first of many raids along the coasts and up the rivers of Europe. Houses and churches were plundered, people were taken as slaves, and the Vikings demanded money before they would leave.

Warriors

Each warrior provided his own armour. Some could afford strong mail armour, others made do with a leather tunic. But most wore pointed iron helmets and carried a round wooden shield.

Double-edged blade

Weaponry

Most Viking warriors fought with swords or axes, although spears and bows were also used. Iron swords were the most important weapons.

Conquests

The Vikings defeated some of the most powerful people in Europe, such as King Edmund of East Anglia, who was tortured and killed when he refused to give up Christianity.

Traders

Viking traders brought to Britain and the Mediterranean items such as furs, whalebone, walrus ivory, and timber. They brought back wheat and cloth from Britain, and pots and wine from the Mediterranean.

Coins

Most Viking traders worked by barter – exchanging goods from their homeland for items they wanted. Then coins came into use and, by the end of the 10th century, they were being widely used.

Furs

The Vikings traded animal products that could only be found in the north. Walrus hide could be turned into ropes and leather. The fur of animals such as brown bears and wolves made warm clothes.

Brown bear

Grey wolf

Seal

Weights

The Vikings developed a system of weights and measures. These five pieces would have been used to weigh small items, such as jewellery made from precious metals. The largest weighs around 40 g (1.4 oz).

Iron weights

Arts and jewellery

Rich people wore brooches, arm-bands, rings, and gold or silver pendants. Poorer people wore bronze or pewter jewellery.

Gripping beast brooch

Silver spiral arm-ring

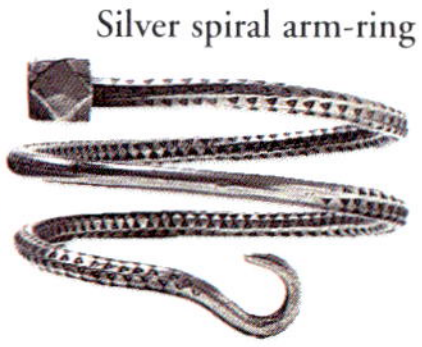

Leif Ericsson

In about the year 1000 Leif Ericsson (born c.970) sailed to North America, and explored the coast, spending the winter in a place he named Vinland (wine land) after the grapes he found there. He was following up the accidental discovery of North America in 986 by a fellow Viking, Bjarni Herjolfsson, who was blown off-course on a voyage from Iceland to Greenland.

FIND OUT MORE
ARCHAEOLOGY
EXPLORATION
NAVIGATION
SCANDINAVIA, HISTORY OF
SHIPS AND BOATS

Vikings

Everyday objects

Hnefatafl was a popular Viking board game.

Nine men's morris is still played today in some places.

Glassware was used only by the richest Vikings because it was so difficult to get. Many jugs and cups were found in graves in Sweden.

Purses and pouches were an everyday necessity.

Weapons and body armor

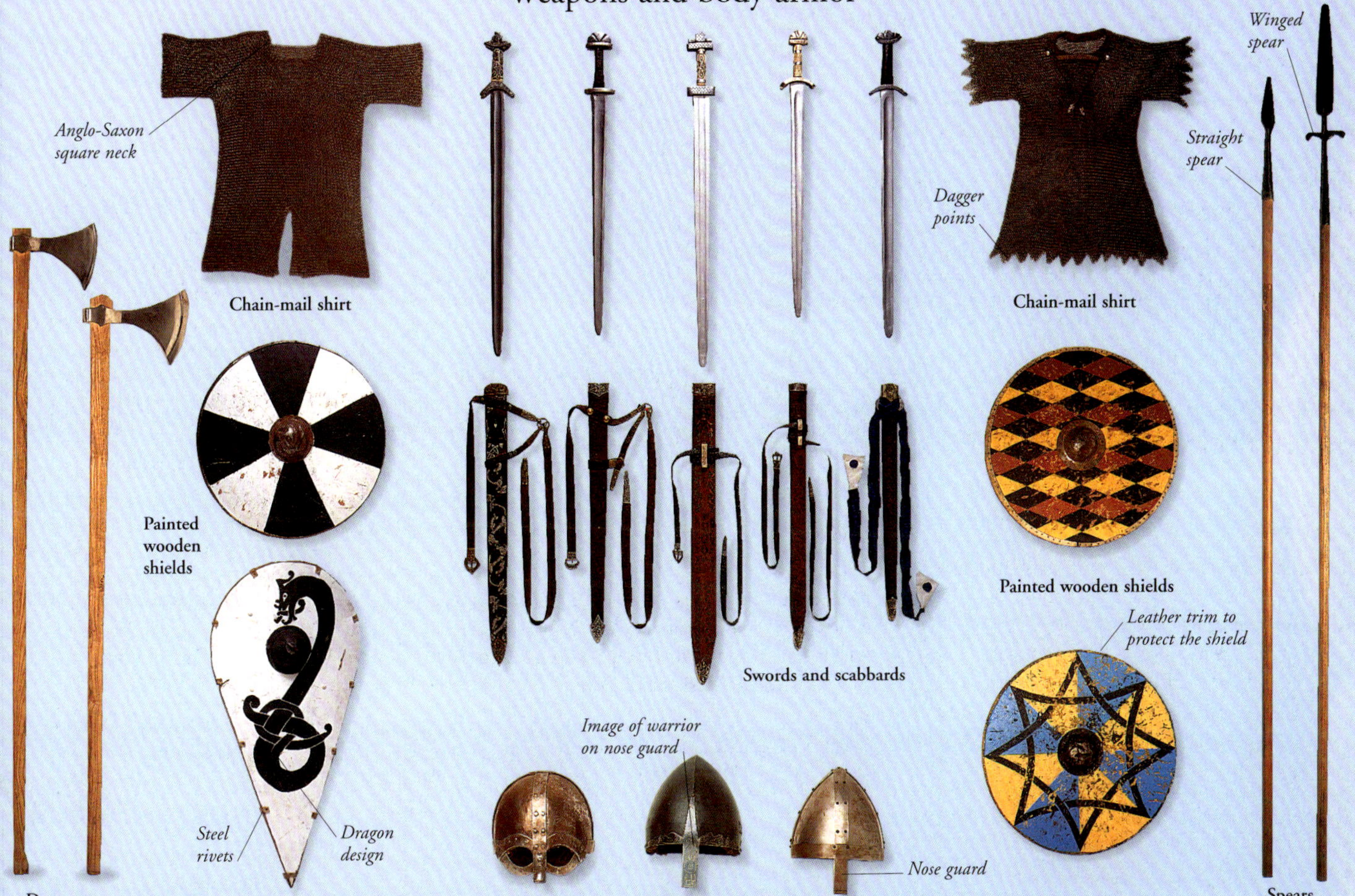

Chain-mail shirt

Chain-mail shirt

Painted wooden shields

Painted wooden shields

Swords and scabbards

Dane axes

Helmets

Spears

Jewelry

Gripping beast brooch

Trefoil brooch

Swedish disk brooch

Oval brooch

Brooches were mainly used to fasten cloaks.

Disk pendant

Comb pendant

Cross pendant

Dwarf pendant

Pendants were often made of gold and silver for the rich, and bronze and pewter for the poor.

Men's jewelry, such as this necklace, was often highly decorative.

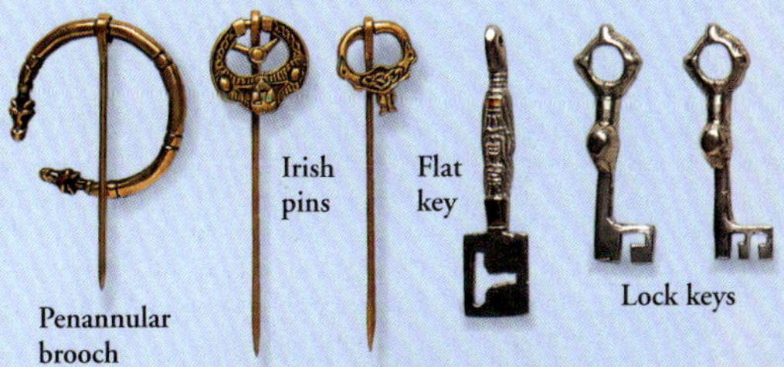

Penannular brooch

Lock keys

Birka man

Odin's head

Valkyrie

Birka crucifix

Pendants could show pagan symbols, such as Odin's head or the Valkyrie, or Christian, such as the crucifix.

VOLCANOES

THE ERUPTION OF A volcano can be one of nature's most terrifying events. A volcano is a vent or fissure where magma (molten rock) from the Earth's hot interior emerges onto the surface. In some places, the molten rock, called lava once it has emerged on to the surface, oozes out slowly and gently. But in others, the eruption is a violent explosion, flinging out molten lava, red-hot lumps of rock, scorching ash, and clouds of steam which spread for kilometres.

Volcanic eruptions

Volcanoes erupt violently when the build-up of magma in the magma chamber below creates enough pressure to blast through the clogged vent. This sudden release of pressure causes a rapid expansion of bubbles of carbon dioxide gas that remains dissolved in the magma while it is under pressure. This expansion creates fountains of lava that stream from the volcano's vent.

Volcanic phases

All volcanoes, on land and under the sea, are at different stages in their life cycles. Some volcanoes are very active, erupting year after year. Others are dormant (sleeping) and erupt only once in a while. Many more are extinct – meaning they have stopped erupting altogether. Vulcanologists monitor active and dormant volcanoes to try to predict future eruptions.

Extinct
Once a volcano is extinct, it will begin to be eroded by wind and weather. All that remains of this extinct volcano in Le Puy, France, is the hard plug of material that once clogged the volcano's vent.

Active
Some volcanoes erupt almost continuously, while others erupt very violently but only at infrequent intervals. Each year there are about 25 major volcanic eruptions on land and thousands of minor ones.

Types of volcano

Volcanoes are of different shapes and sizes, depending on the thickness of their lava and the shape of their vents.

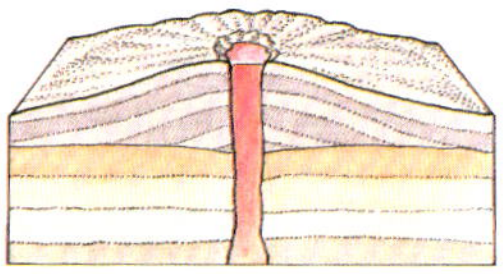

Shield volcanoes are broad, shallow cones made of very runny lava that flows easily.

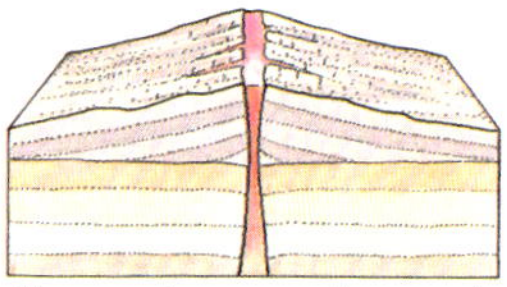

Fissure volcanoes are long cracks in the ground through which the magma oozes up gently.

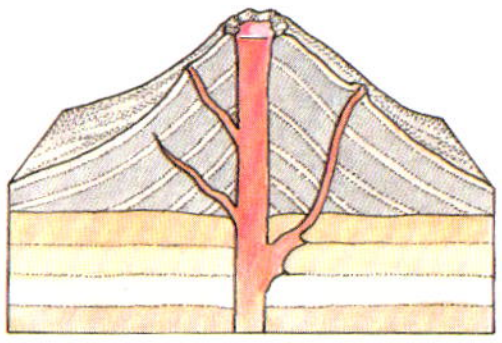

Composite cones are built up of alternate layers of lava and ash. Cones can be made of ash alone.

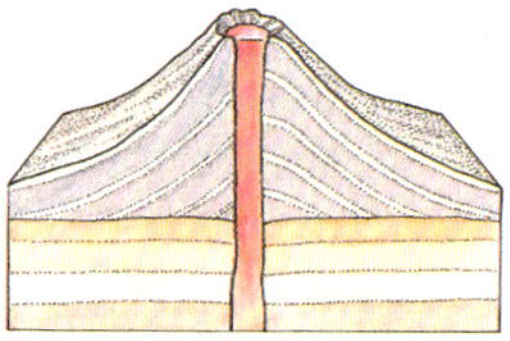

Ash and cinder volcanoes have concave-shaped cones made of the solid fragments ejected by eruptions.

Katia and Maurice Krafft

French vulcanologists Maurice Krafft (1946–91) and Katia Krafft (1947–91) were legendary for working consistently closer to erupting volcanoes than any other vulcanologists. They obtained unique data, amazing film footage, and close-up photographs of eruptions. Sadly, their bravery led to their deaths. In 1991 they were engulfed by a Japanese volcano. Their bodies were never found.

Types of lava

Lava is the molten rock thrown out by a volcano. The most common forms of lava are basalt, which is thin and runny, and cools to a heavy, black rock, and rhyolite, a thick, pale, biscuit-coloured lava. How a volcano erupts depends on the lava's thickness.

Acidic
Very viscous lava flows such as this one are usually linked to acidic magma, which contains a high proportion of the mineral silica.

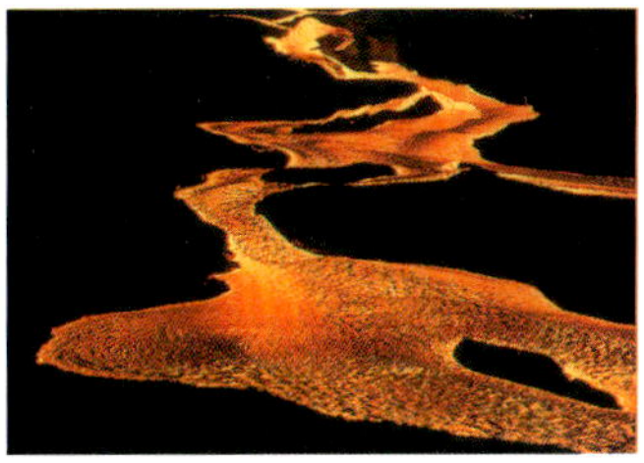

Aa
In Hawaii, where Mauna Loa is erupting almost all the time, lava that solidifies into sharp jagged chunks is known as aa, or block lava. Lava in this part of the world is basic, which means it is non-acidic.

Pahoehoe
Lava may cool quickly to form a skin tough enough to walk over. If lava continues to flow underneath, the surface wrinkles into rope-like coils. In Hawaii this is called pahoehoe, or corded lava.

Pyroclastic debris

When an explosive volcano blasts out the plug of volcanic material in its vent, the plug is shattered into an array of fragments. These fragments are known as pyroclasts, which means "fire-broken".

Ashfalls
Big volcanic eruptions can fling vast clouds of ash and dust high into the sky. These can often fall like snow, covering the ground for far around in a thick grey blanket.

Tephra
Tephra are chunks of pyroclastic rock that are thrown high into the air during an eruption and rattle down on the slopes below.

Volcanic bombs
Pyroclastic fragments over 32 mm (1.26 in) across are known as volcanic bombs. They take various forms including "breadcrust bombs" (above).

Lapilli
Lapilli are smaller chunks of tephra. Sometimes they are foam-like magma fragments; sometimes they are more solid lithic (rock) pieces.

Pele's hair
Lava in Hawaii is so fluid that it forms long strands as it is flung out. This is known as Pele's hair, after the Hawaiian goddess of volcanoes.

Volcanic landscape

In volcanic areas, underground heat may create other effects on the surface as well as volcanoes. Hot gases may billow out through fissures, for instance, while the heat of rocks underground may be enough to boil groundwater, creating jets of water or bubbling mud pools.

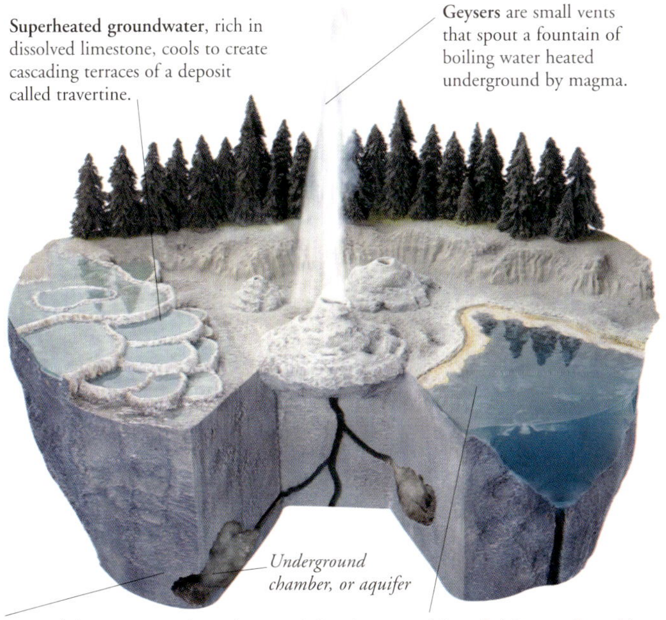

Volcanic features

Volcanoes and volcanic activity leave behind all kinds of distinctive features in the landscape to bear witness to their ferocity and heat – sometimes relics of the outpouring of lava, sometimes relics of their effect on landscape features.

Calderas
Calderas are saucer-like craters at the tops of volcanic cones, created by the collapse of the cone during a huge explosion. Smaller calderas can occur when the top of a volcano is blown off by an eruption.

Giant's Causeway
The extraordinary hexagonal, basaltic columns that make up the Giant's Causeway in Co. Antrim, Northern Ireland, are formed of cooled lava from ancient volcanic activity.

Cones
The most distinctive volcanic relic is a cone-shaped mountain built up as lava which poured out from the vent and is then covered by ash. This process continues in successive eruptions.

FIND OUT MORE
CONTINENTS | EARTH | EARTHQUAKES | FOSSILS | MOUNTAINS AND VALLEYS | ROCKS AND MINERALS | ROMAN EMPIRE

WARFARE

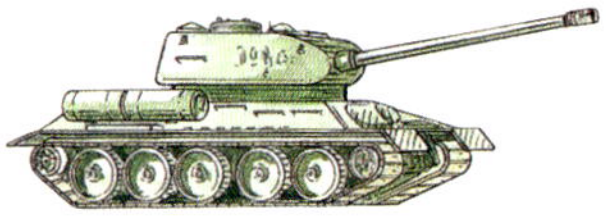

WHEN PEOPLE DISAGREE about land, property, religion, or politics, one person may end the argument with violence. When nations cannot agree, the violence takes the form of warfare. If one nation is very strong, warfare can seem like an easy way of winning land or resources. But battles kill so many people, and cost so much, that nations usually start fighting only when diplomacy has failed. Peacekeeping organizations, such as the United Nations, aim to keep diplomacy working and stop wars before they begin.

Ancient warfare

Battles are part of every country's history. Some past civilizations glorified war as a means to make their nation strong. However, ancient wars were often smaller and less destructive; without modern industry and transport, it was more difficult to supply a huge army with weapons and food.

Stirrups

Technology decided the winner in ancient wars, as it does today. From at least the 4th century AD, Chinese horsemen were equipped with stirrups. Well-balanced in the saddle, they easily defeated enemies without stirrups.

Tomb figure of warrior

Modern warfare

As science and industry flourished and farms grew more food in the 19th century, European nations devised more awful forms of war. Inventions such as the machine gun could kill more soldiers; with better transport, armies could fight in more distant regions, and food surpluses meant troops rarely starved. In this "total war", everyone who could either fought or supplied troops.

World war

During the 20th centuy, warfare became truly global for the first time. World Wars I and II involved almost every nation. Countries taking part made military service compulsory, and poured all their resources into the conflicts. As well as using armies and navies, each side waged war against civilians and economic targets in order to break down the will to fight on.

Allied bombs devastated Dresden, Germany, in February 1945.

The ancient city was of no military value.

Guerilla organization flag, Cameroon

Civil war

In a civil war, groups within the same state fight each other. They battle for racial or religious reasons, or to control the government. Since the end of World War II in 1945, most wars that have broken out have been civil wars.

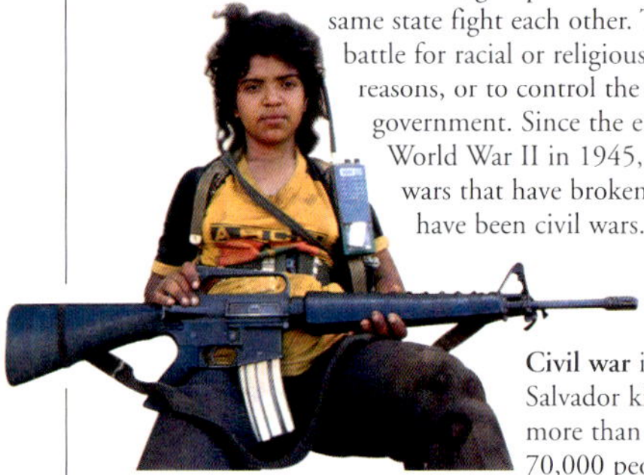

Civil war in El Salvador killed more than 70,000 people.

Guerilla war

Troops who occupy enemy lands may face guerilla (little war) soldiers. Guerillas often succeed, despite poor equipment and little training, because they know the countryside and have the support of local people.

US soldiers in Vietnam

Limited war

Some modern wars, such as the Vietnam War (1957–75) or the Iran-Iraq conflict (1980–88), are confined to a small region. These limited wars may not spread, because allies of the warring nations have little to gain by joining in, and much to lose.

Where war happens

A military leader must choose the battlefield with care. Each side's weapons, communications, and logistics (their ability to keep fighters fed, clothed, and armed) decide what makes a favourable battlefield for them, and a bad one for the enemy.

Infantry soldiers

On land

A major goal in war is to occupy the territory of a neighbour, so most wars are fought partly on land. However, because of the power of modern aircraft, armies must now control the skies before they can advance on the ground.

Karl von Clausewitz

Von Clausewitz (1780–1831) was a Prussian general. His influential book On War set out his theories on the nature of war and the tactics needed to win. It defined war as "an act of violence intended to compel our opponent to fulfil our will".

At sea

When all long-distance transport was by ship, warring nations battled to control the seas. Air transport has now made naval battles less important. Battleships and aircraft carriers are easy targets for missiles, so navies hide much of their power beneath the waves, in submarines.

German U-boat shells a merchant vessel, World War II.

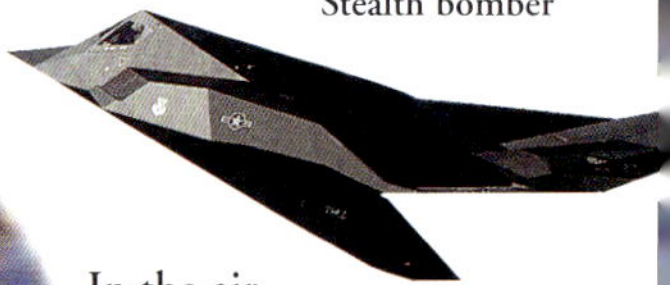

Stealth bomber

In the air

War first spread to the air in World War I (1914–1918). Radar and missile systems now provide defences against bombers and fighter planes, but methods of attack have also improved: the "stealth" bomber cannot be detected by radar.

W

The rules of war

Formal rules to protect ordinary soldiers and civilians during war were first attempted in 1863, when the German-American scholar Francis Lieber (1800–1872) wrote *Code for the Government of Armies in the Field.* His work recognized the need to ban weapons that caused unnecessary suffering, and to protect the wounded and prisoners of war; it influenced later international agreements about the conduct of warfare.

Geneva Convention

Henri Dunant (1828–1910), a Swiss citizen, founded the Red Cross to relieve the suffering of war wounded. In 1864, a Convention protecting them and those treating them was signed in Geneva by European nations; later treaties have extended its protection.

International Red Cross logo

Nürnberg

After World War II, Nazi leaders were tried at a special court at Nürnberg, Germany, for the murder of more than six million people (mostly Jews). The court convicted 22 Nazis of breaking international treaties and the rules of war, and of crimes against humanity.

Prisoners of war

In the past, prisoners of war (POWs) became slaves, or bought their freedom, but the Geneva Convention now protects them. An army that captures uniformed enemy soldiers must move them away from the battlefield and imprison them in reasonable conditions until the war ends.

Boer women as prisoners of war

The cost of war

In war each side fears defeat so much that no price seems too high to pay for victory. Though the defeated side generally suffers more, the cost of winning can also be disabling. War costs are measured not just financially, but also in the loss of natural resources and human lives. During the 20th century, more than 100 million soldiers and non-combatants have been killed in wars.

The Unknown Soldier

Burying the body of an unidentified soldier in a special Tomb of the Unknown Soldier created a memorial to all the nameless war dead.

Refugees

When wars drive civilians across borders to seek asylum (a place of safety) they become refugees. They have no rights, and often no money or possessions. For food, water, shelter and medical care many depend on the country sheltering them, or on organizations such as the United Nations.

In the 1990s, war forced 4.5 million Sudanese to leave their homes.

Environmental damage

Wildlife and the natural environment always suffer in and around a battle zone. Sometimes, nations may use environmental damage as a weapon: in the Vietnam War, US forces deliberately killed crops and jungle to deny their enemy food and cover. Weapons testing, and the pressure that refugees put on the land as they try to survive, also severely damage the environment.

Bomb damage

War dead

War kills and injures huge numbers of servicemen and women; during World War I about 8.5 million servicemen died. But the changing nature of warfare meant that by World War II more civilians were killed than soldiers. In war today, bombs and bullets kill some; hunger and disease kill many more.

World War I graves in France

Government war bonds promise interest on loans.

Paying for war

War consumes a huge share of a nation's wealth: in 1944, for example, the British government spent 60 percent of its people's earnings on World War II. Governments may pay for war with borrowed money, which later generations repay.

Timeline

1096–9 European Christian knights win control of Palestine, the Holy Land, in the first, and most successful, Crusade (holy war) against the Arab world.

1240 Mongol warriors from central Asia capture Kiyyev (Kiev), Ukraine, in one of a series of wars that give them control of much of Asia and eastern Europe.

Mongol quiver

1861–5 In a bloody Civil War, northern and southern American states fight with modern weapons and supplies. The north wins; more than 600,000 people die.

1914–18 Thirty countries fight for control of Europe. Millions die in World War I.

1939–45 In World War II, more fighters die than in all previous wars put together.

1957–75 US fights a damaging war in Vietnam.

1967 The Six-Day War is fought between Israel and Arab forces. Israel wins.

The Nazis forced Jews to wear yellow stars as identity badges.

1990–91 A US-led alliance defeats Iraq in the Gulf War.

2001–02 September 11 terrorism leads to US-led war on Afghanistan.

2001–02 US-led coalition deposes Saddam Hussein's regime in Iraq.

FIND OUT MORE
ARMS AND ARMOUR | COLD WAR | GUNS | HOLOCAUST | PEACE MOVEMENTS | UNITED NATIONS | WARPLANES | WARSHIPS | WEAPONS | WORLD WAR I | WORLD WAR II

WARPLANES

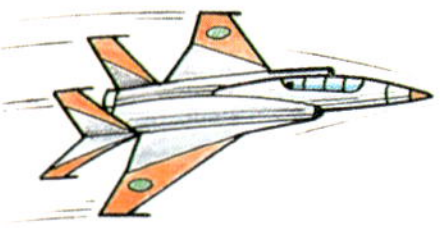

AEROPLANES WERE first used in warfare during World War I (1914–18). They have been vital elements of armed combat ever since. Warplanes range from fast, nimble, jet-powered fighters to battlefield helicopters and tankers for in-flight refuelling. Between them, they find and destroy enemy aircraft and targets on the ground. Warplanes also help transport troops and equipment to and from the battlefield. In peacetime, military transport aircraft often help with emergencies and famine relief.

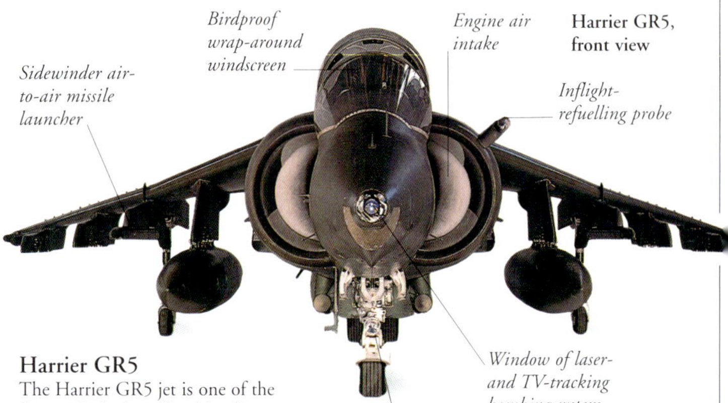

Harrier GR5, front view

Harrier GR5
The Harrier GR5 jet is one of the few vertical take-off and landing (VTOL) strike aircraft in operation. It is thrust upwards by the power of jet nozzles which point downwards. It does not need a runway, so can be hidden near to the battlefront.

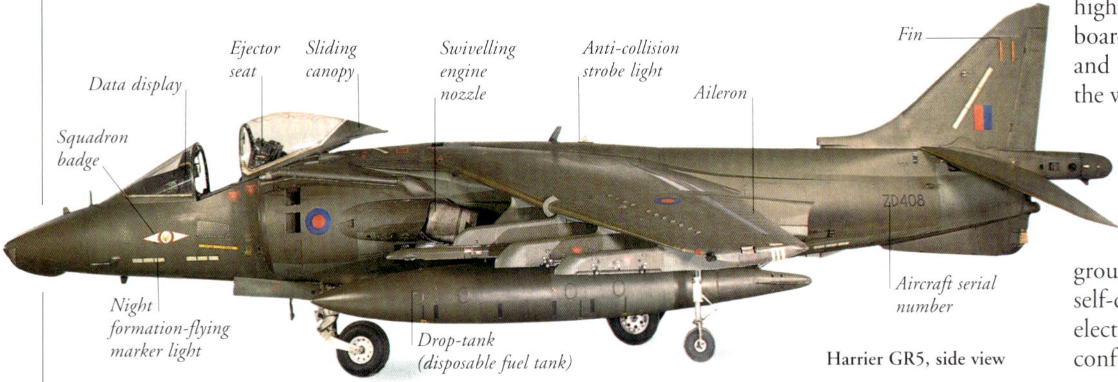

Harrier GR5, side view

Parts of a warplane

Fighters and fighter-bombers are highly sophisticated aircraft. On-board computers help the pilot fly and navigate the aircraft and operate the weapons. Warplanes carry air-to-air weapons (guns and missiles) for attacking other aircraft, and air-to-ground weapons (missiles and bombs) for attacking targets on the ground and at sea. They also have self-defence systems, including electronic beams and flares for confusing missiles fired at them.

Types of warplane

Warplanes are either combat aircraft or non-combat aircraft, which support other military forces. Combat aircraft include fighters (also called interceptors), which win superiority in the air, enabling other aircraft to operate over a battlezone, bombers, and fighter-bombers. Non-combat aircraft carry out reconnaissance, or carry troops and equipment rapidly to a battle zone.

Rockwell B-1B

Heavy bombers
Heavy bombers are large aircraft, often as big as passenger airliners. They fly high above the battlefield and release bombs, which fall to the ground. Several crew members are needed to operate the aircraft.

Cobra Venom AH-1W

Attack helicopters
A cross between helicopters and fighter aircraft, these destroy enemy targets on the battlefield with a cannon, rockets, and missiles.

Heavy-lift aircraft
Heavy-lift aircraft (right) carry hundreds of fully-equipped military personnel from home bases to a war zone.

Lockheed C5 Galaxy

Boeing E3A

Reconnaissance aircraft
Keeping track of enemy positions is the job of reconnaissance aircraft (left). Some fly low and fast, taking photographs. Others fly high, using powerful radar to detect other aircraft.

Air forces

An air force is much more than just a collection of aircraft and their crews. There are thousands of ground staff too, including the engineers who service the aircraft. Most air forces are divided into sections called squadrons. The first organized air force was the British Royal Air Force (RAF), formed in 1918.

Uniform, jet crew member, British RAF

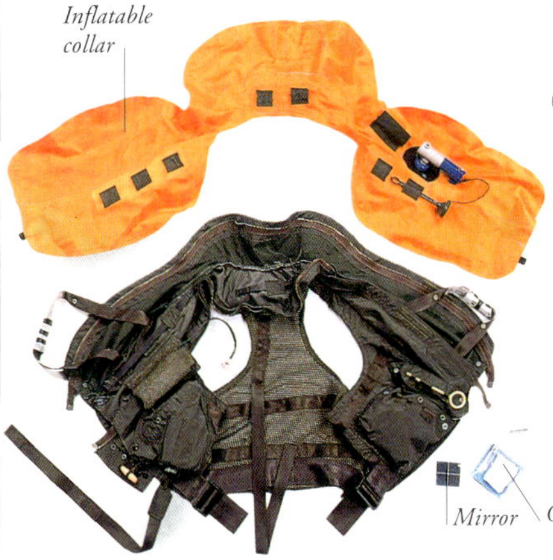

Jet crew wear life-jackets with survival aids, in case they need to eject from a plane.

FIND OUT MORE
AIRCRAFT | AIRSHIPS AND BALLOONS | ARMIES | ENGINES AND MOTORS | FLIGHT, HISTORY OF | WARFARE | WEAPONS | WORLD WAR I | WORLD WAR II

WARSHIPS

SEVERAL DIFFERENT TYPES OF SHIP are involved in modern warfare, from small, fast patrol boats to massive aircraft carriers. Each type carries out a particular job, such as protecting merchant ships from attack or searching for enemy ships and submarines. A modern warship is crammed with sophisticated navigation and weapon systems. Warships normally operate together in groups called fleets. They are supported by naval auxiliary ships, which deliver supplies such as fuel and food.

Parts of a warship

Warships are designed to be fast and easy to manoeuvre. They have lightweight aluminium hulls and powerful gas-turbine engines. Inside, each ship is divided into watertight sections that can be sealed off if the hull is holed during an attack. Here are the crew's quarters, store rooms, and control rooms. Above the deck are weapons and communication equipment. Warships carry several different types of weapons, including guns, missiles, and torpedoes.

Frigate
A frigate is a medium-sized, light, fast warship. Frigates normally escort aircraft carriers, protecting them from attack. They carry anti-aircraft and anti-ship missiles, and submarine hunting equipment.

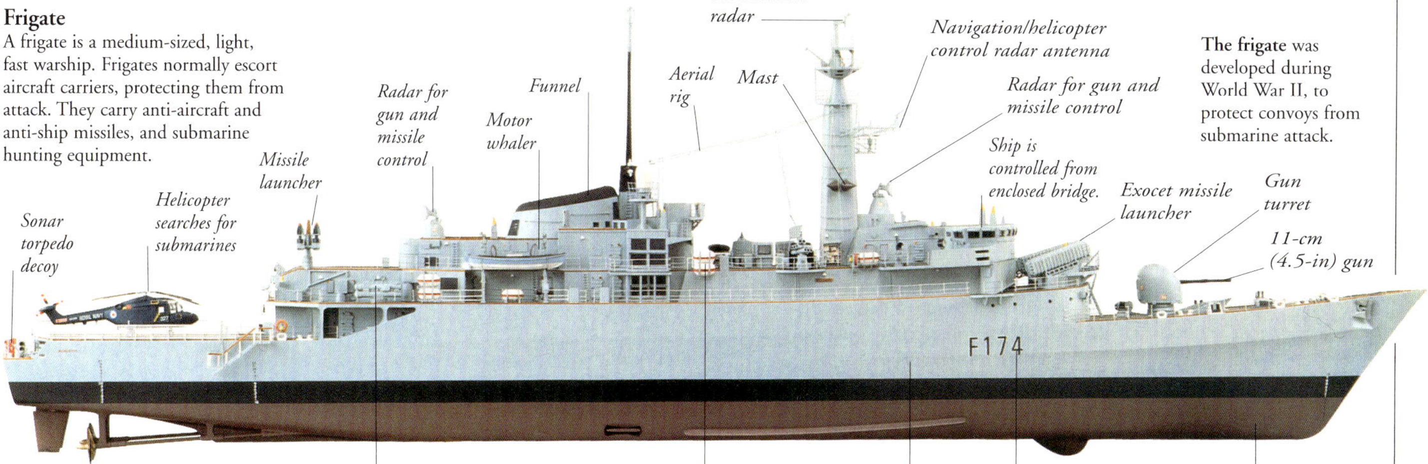

The frigate was developed during World War II, to protect convoys from submarine attack.

Types of warship

Warships are either surface warships or submarines. The most important surface warship is the aircraft carrier. Other types of surface ships defend carriers and attack enemy ships. Submarines are either hunter-killers, which search for and destroy enemy ships, or ballistic missile submarines, which stay hidden in the oceans for months.

US Navy aircraft carrier

German Navy minesweeper

Aircraft carriers
The aircraft carrier is the largest of all warships. It is a floating air base: as well as runways for take-offs and landings, it has hangars where planes are serviced, and a control tower to communicate with pilots. The largest aircraft carriers carry up to 100 airplanes and a crew of more than 2,000 sailors, plus a flying crew of more than 1,000.

Mine warfare vessels
Minehunters search for mines (explosive charges) sunk beneath the sea; minesweepers have special equipment to locate and destroy surface mines. These warships have wood or plastic hulls, because magnetic mines are set off when a steel hull comes near them.

Helicopter cruisers
Cruisers are large warships, armed with guns, missiles, and torpedoes. A helicopter cruiser has a deck at the rear where helicopters land, and hangers where helicopters are stored.

US Navy helicopter cruiser

Navies

In wartime, a navy's job is to keep a nation's sea lanes open, protect merchant and other ships at sea, hunt and destroy enemy ships, and support armies and air forces. In time of peace, they help with disaster relief and rescue work, and make visits to foreign countries to promote goodwill.

Uniforms
This uniform from the Soviet Navy is in a traditional style. Many nations have a similar uniform.

Jumper, shirt, collar

Trousers

Cap

Boots

FIND OUT MORE
Armies
Radar and Sonar
Sailing and other Watersports
Ships and Boats
Submarines
Transport, History of
Warfare
Weapons
World War II

WASHINGTON, GEORGE

As leader of the American forces that won the Revolutionary War against the British and as the first president of the new nation, George Washington is known as the "Father of his Country". He learned his military skills fighting for the British in the 1750s, and used those skills to good effect against them 20 years later. A fine politician and administrator, he worked hard to unite his new country and to reconcile conflicting interests. His honesty and moderation made him a symbol of his nation.

Early life

Washington was born in 1732 into a land-owning family in Virginia. When he was 11 his father died, and he went to live with his half-brother Lawrence. George wanted to go to sea, but was persuaded to train as a surveyor. A practical man, he succeeded despite his limited education.

Musket from the French-Indian War

French-Indian War

In 1753, French armies from Canada occupied the Ohio River Valley. George Washington fought for the British against the Frenchand their native American allies. He was promoted quickly for his military and organizational skills.

Mount Vernon

When his half-brother Lawrence died in 1752, George inherited the family's large estate of Mount Vernon, Virginia. He made many changes there and experimented with new crops. In 1759, he married Martha Custis, a wealthy widow, and entered Virginian politics. Throughout Washington's life, Mount Vernon was a welcome retreat, and he retired there at the end of his life.

Delegates at the Continental Congress

Continental Congress

Washington was an early champion of American independence. In 1774 and 1775, he served as a delegate from Virginia to the Continental Congresses held to organize the 13 colonies' struggle against the British. When the Revolutionary War broke out in 1775, the Congress appointed Washington commander-in-chief of the colonial army.

Washington Crossing The Delaware by Emanuel Leutze

Commander-in-chief

When war broke out in 1775, Washington took over a disorganized, ill-equipped army incapable of beating the professional, well-equipped British. Despite interference from Congress, he turned the colonial troops into an efficient force, able to outwit and defeat the British in 1781.

Trenton

In the first two years of the war, American troops were outmanoeuvred by the British. On 25 December 1776, Washington and his troops crossed the ice-bound Delaware River near Trenton, New Jersey. They captured the surprised British army the next day at the Battle of Trenton.

Valley Forge

The American army spent the winter of 1777–78 in Valley Forge, Pennsylvania. The winter was severe and food and clothing were scarce, but despite desertions and the threat of mutiny, Washington showed his grit and determination, holding his army together. In the spring, the army emerged well-prepared for battle.

President of the United States

After American independence was assured in 1783, Washington withdrew from politics. But conflicts between the states led to him taking a leading role. In 1787, he presided over the convention which drafted the constitution, and in 1789 was unanimously elected president of the new country. He served two four-year terms before retiring in 1797.

Thomas Jefferson

The author of the American Constitution, Thomas Jefferson (1743–1826) became secretary of state under Washington and led the Democratic-Republicans, who favoured individual and state rights. Washington tried to keep aloof from party politics but favoured the Federalists, who wanted a stronger national state. Party conflicts caused many problems during Washington's presidency.

Whiskey Rebellion

In 1794, rioting broke out against the imposition of a national tax on alcoholic drink. The American government tried to enforce the law, but in the end Washington was forced to use troops. This, and other troubles, meant that Washington decided against running for a third term as president.

George Washington

- 1732 Born in Virginia.
- 1743 On the death of his father, goes to live with his brother Lawrence.
- 1754–59 Fights in the British Army against the French.
- 1759 Enters Virginia politics.
- 1774–75 Delegate at two Continental Congresses.
- 1775 Appointed commander-in-chief of Colonial forces.
- 1783 USA wins independence from Britain.
- 1789–97 Serves two terms as President of the USA.
- 1799 Dies at Mount Vernon.

FIND OUT MORE
American Revolution
Governments and Politics
Law
United States, History of

WEAPONS

STRENGTH AND SKILL decide the winner in a fight without weapons, but in armed combat, the fighter with the better killing tool may win. Ever since people began to compete for land or food, warriors have sought weapons of increasing power. Changing technology supplied them: metals were used to make swords; nuclear power was first used in bombs. This arms race has now led to weapons so powerful that a nation that used them might win the war, but would destroy everything in the conquered lands.

Early weapons

Early warriors fought with clubs and short blades. Lances and spears kept the enemy farther away; missiles such as the boomerang allowed warriors to attack anyone within throwing distance. To launch missiles further still, fighters used slingshots or bows.

The dagger, used in hand-to-hand fighting, was one of the first weapons.

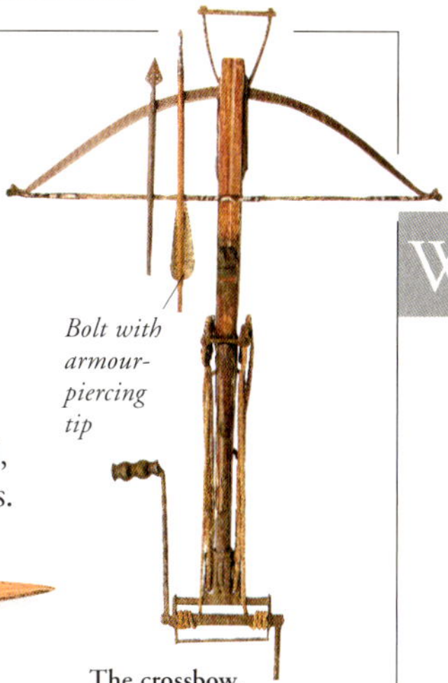

The crossbow, a powerful weapon used in medieval warfare.

Gunpowder

Gunpowder

The most far-reaching development in weapons technology came in the 14th century, with the invention of firearms. These weapons were powered by gunpowder, an explosive. Although feeble at first, firearms were soon capable of firing missiles great distances. Battles could be fought at long range, instead of face-to-face.

Nikolaus von Dreyse

German gunsmith Dreyse (1787–1867) designed a more effective weapon for the battlefield: a rifle that fired twice as fast as earlier guns. Troops loaded bullets near the trigger so they could shoot lying down, safe from enemy fire. The Prussian army began using the gun in 1840.

Booby traps

Seemingly harmless objects or areas can be unexpectedly deadly. Guerilla fighters may capture or wound enemies with trip wires or spike-filled holes. Most modern traps rely on explosives. Buried anti-tank mines explode when vehicles crush them; smaller anti-personnel (AP) mines blast people treading on them. Aircraft can drop huge numbers of AP mines very quickly.

How an AP mine works

When someone treads on an AP mine, the pressure sets off a process that detonates an explosive charge. The force of the explosion travels upwards, causing terrible injuries. Such mines are designed to maim rather than kill, as a wounded person needs more care than a dead one, draining enemy resources.

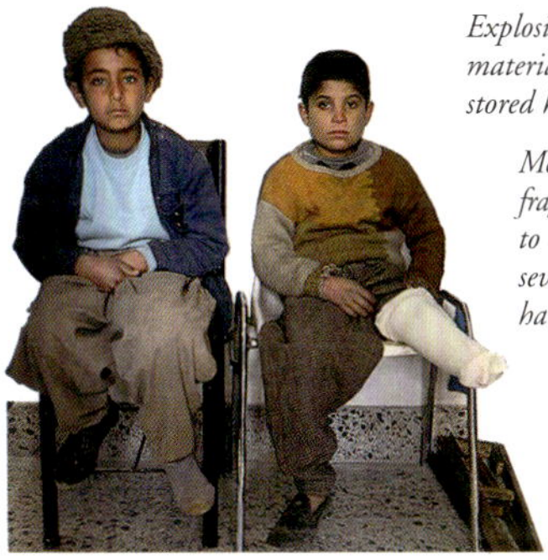

Mine victims, Kurdistan, 1993

AP mine, World War II

Bombs and missiles

A bomb is a container filled with explosive material and a detonator to make it explode. The explosion causes a lethal blast, scattering deadly bits of the bomb casing far and wide. Missiles are weapons that are propelled towards a target; they allow a warring nation to destroy an enemy nation without risking the life of a single soldier.

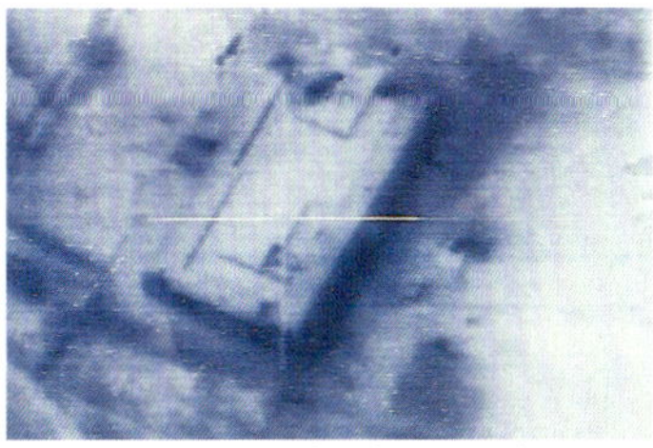

Smart bomb approaches target.

Smart bombs

"Smart" bombs are missiles in which a warhead is guided directly to its target by a laser-aiming device or on-board computer map. Some contain video cameras in their noses.

Aerial bombing in World War I: bombs were originally dropped by hand.

Gravity bombs

Dropped from aircraft, gravity bombs contain high exlosive. Most explode when they hit the ground. Modern types may divide into many "bomblets" to blast a wider area.

Mass destruction

The most powerful weapons can destroy a city or poison the land of a whole nation. These weapons are so dangerous that there are international treaties which aim to outlaw their use in war, or at least reduce their numbers.

Nuclear weapons testing, 1995

Nuclear weapons

In an atomic bomb, a sugar-cube-size piece of uranium has the same destructive power as a block of conventional explosive as big as a house.

Chemical weapons

Chemical and biological weapons spread poisons or epidemic diseases, so they kill or injure the enemy without damaging property. Casualties die slowly, overwhelming an enemy's medical facilities.

FIND OUT MORE

ARMS AND ARMOUR · GUNS · HUNDRED YEARS WAR · NUCLEAR POWER · PEACE MOVEMENTS · WARFARE · WORLD WAR I · WORLD WAR II

Weapons

Without gunpowder

War hammer

Arrowheads, c.2700–1800 BC

Dagger (jambiya), of Arab origin

Fighting boomerangs

Samurai sword and scabbard

Tomahawk

Sword bayonet

English longbow and arrow

Metal mace, for attacking armour

Firearms

Rifle, effective at 275 m (900 ft), early 19th century

Silenced Sten submachine gun, World War II

Early pistol, muzzle-loading

6.5 mm type-97 rifle, used by snipers

Colt Commando Carbine, a short, light rifle

Assault rifle, with grenade launcher

Colt Peacemaker revolver

Colt pocket pistol

Taisho automatic pistol, modified for use in Arctic

Liberator pistol, World War II

Heckler and Koch automatic pistol

Tanks, bombs, and missiles

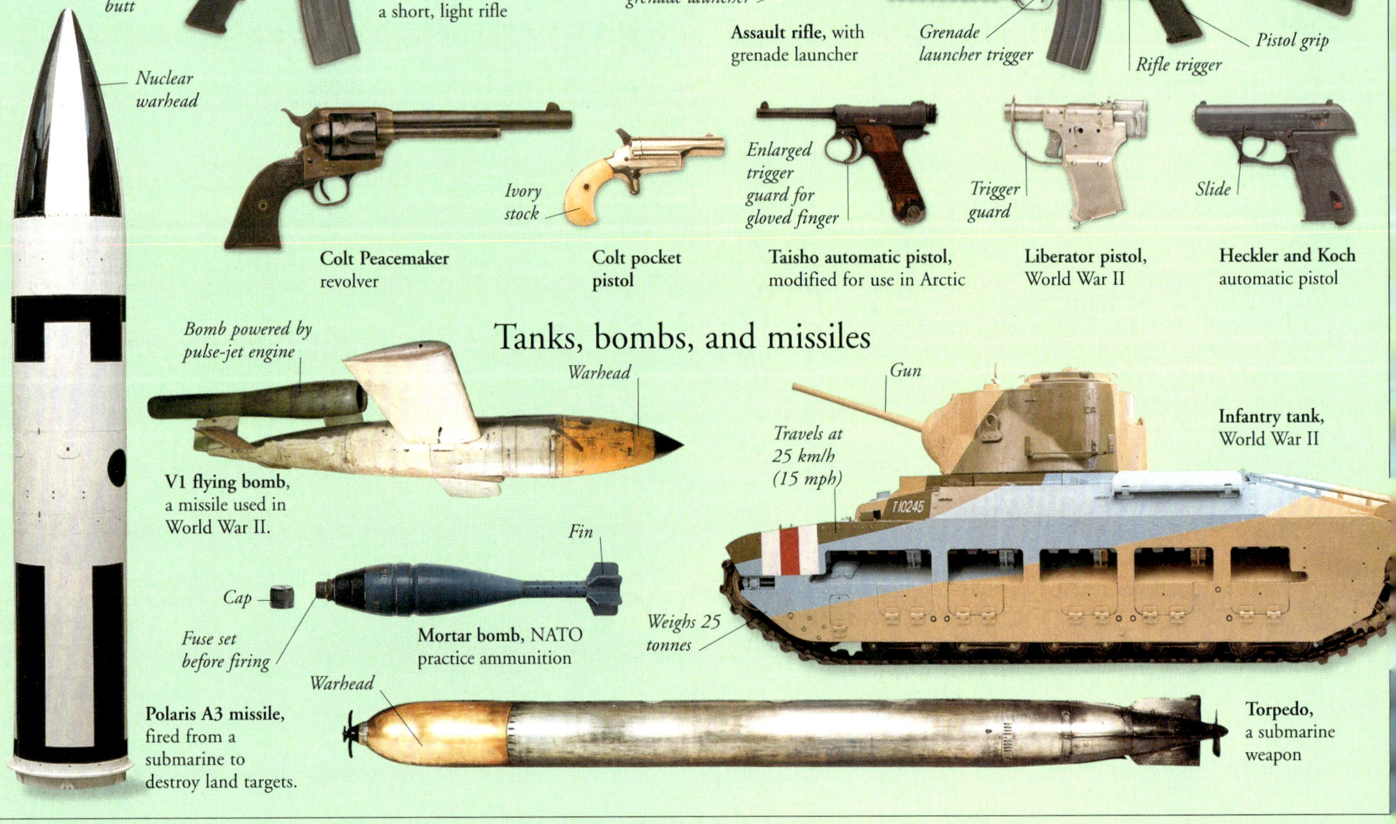

V1 flying bomb, a missile used in World War II.

Infantry tank, World War II

Mortar bomb, NATO practice ammunition

Polaris A3 missile, fired from a submarine to destroy land targets.

Torpedo, a submarine weapon

WEASELS AND MARTENS

SMALL AND SLENDER mammals, weasels and martens are some of the most efficient hunters. They have a fierce reputation and, on their own, can kill prey much larger than themselves. With their excellent senses of smell, hearing, and sight, they track down their prey, then pounce, and kill it with a lethal bite. Different species occupy habitats from the polar regions to the tropics. Some live in trees, others in burrows or among rocks or tree roots.

Young weasels
Weasels breed in the spring, producing litters of up to eight young. The baby weasels stay in the safety of the den in the first weeks of life, and are looked after by the female alone. After about two months, the young begin to hunt for themselves.

Common weasel
One of the most widespread weasels is the common weasel. It weaves through the undergrowth searching for small rodents, such as mice and voles, and is small and lithe enough to pursue them into their burrows. Males may be twice as big as females so they chase larger prey down larger burrows. Each weasel has its own territory, which may cover several hectares.

Weasels

Stoats, polecats, minks, weasels, and ferrets are all types of weasel. They have long, sinuous bodies, long necks, and short legs. Mostly nocturnal hunters, they can move extremely fast and run, climb, and swim after their prey.

Weasels have a flexible spine and strong back muscles.

Weasels are particularly good at hearing high-pitched sounds, such as a mouse squeaking.

Short legs allow the weasel to manoeuvre in small burrows.

All weasels stand up on their back legs to look around.

Stoat
The stoat, seen here tracking its prey by scent, looks similar to the common weasel, but it has a black tip to its tail and is a little bigger than the weasel. It can tackle prey as large as a hare. In the northern, colder parts of its range, the stoat's coat turns white in winter to camouflage it against the snow. It is then known as ermine.

Least weasel skull
The least weasel is the smallest carnivore in the world, only 17.5 cm (6.8 in) long. Its strong jaws and sharp stabbing teeth are typical of all weasels.

Polecats are solitary animals, as are all weasels.

Polecats
Like most weasels, polecats are versatile hunters, eating rodents, rabbits, frogs, birds, and lizards. They patrol their territory at night, marking it with their scent.

Minks
These weasels are good swimmers, helped by their partly webbed feet. They usually live by rivers, lakes, and marshes, taking their prey of fish, frogs, and birds from the water.

Minks have thick, oily, waterproof fur.

Martens

There are eight species of marten inhabiting forests in Europe, Asia, Canada, and Alaska. They are larger than weasels, and their slightly longer limbs make them better climbers. They readily catch prey in trees, though they also hunt on the ground, taking squirrels, birds, eggs, insects, and plant food such as berries.

Pine marten
An extremely agile climber, the pine marten is able to run and leap along branches. It has a bushy tail that helps with balance, and long claws and large paws that grip the bark. It is the largest Eurasian marten.

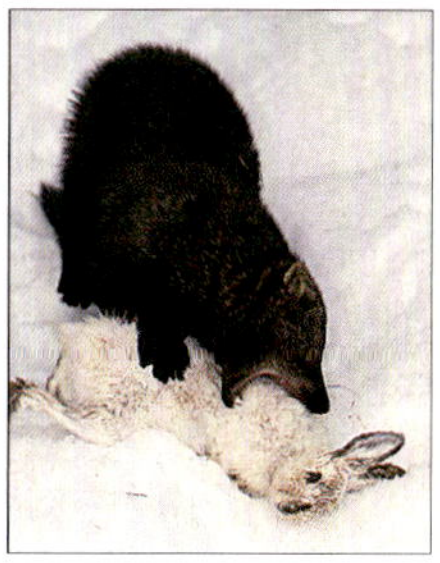

Fisher
Despite its name, the fisher feeds largely on the flesh of birds and small mammals such as rabbits. It is known for its ability to kill porcupines, whose spines it avoids by attacking the unprotected face and belly.

Wolverine
A giant among weasels and martens, the wolverine weighs up to 25 kg (55 lb). It is powerful enough to kill and eat a reindeer. It catches its prey not by stalking, but by pouncing in ambush, often from a tree.

Zorilla
Widespread in Africa, the zorilla's vivid stripes act as a warning to larger predators not to attack. If the warning is ignored, the zorilla will raise its tail and spray a noxious fluid at the attacker.

COMMON WEASEL	
SCIENTIFIC NAME	*Mustela nivalis*
ORDER	Carnivora
FAMILY	Mustelidae
DISTRIBUTION	Europe, most of Asia, northwest Africa
DIET	Rodents, moles, rabbits, birds
SIZE	Length 21–29 cm (8–11.5 in)

FIND OUT MORE: ANIMAL BEHAVIOUR | BADGERS, OTTERS, AND SKUNKS | FOOD WEBS AND CHAINS | MAMMALS

WEATHER

WIND, RAIN, SNOW, fog, frost, and sunshine are all signs of the constant shifting of the lowest level of the atmosphere. This continual change is what we call the weather. The weather changes in four main ways: its movement, which can bring winds; its temperature, which can cause anything from frosts to heat waves; its moisture content, which can bring rain and fog; and its pressure, which can cause anything from cloudless days to fierce storms. The average weather in one particular area is known as the climate.

Highs

These are caused by blocks of denser air in the upper atmosphere. The density of the air makes it heavy, which creates a high pressure region. With very little water vapour in it, a high creates a clear and cloudless day.

Depressions and fronts

The atmosphere often forms into blocks of air, or air masses, over an area where conditions are similar. A front is the boundary between two air masses. Where a warm and cold air mass meet, lighter air rises up over the cold, creating a low pressure zone, or depression. This brings storms as it develops and drifts eastwards.

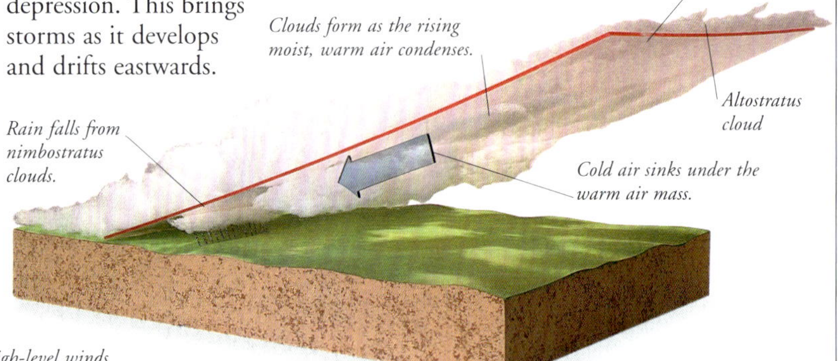

Warm front

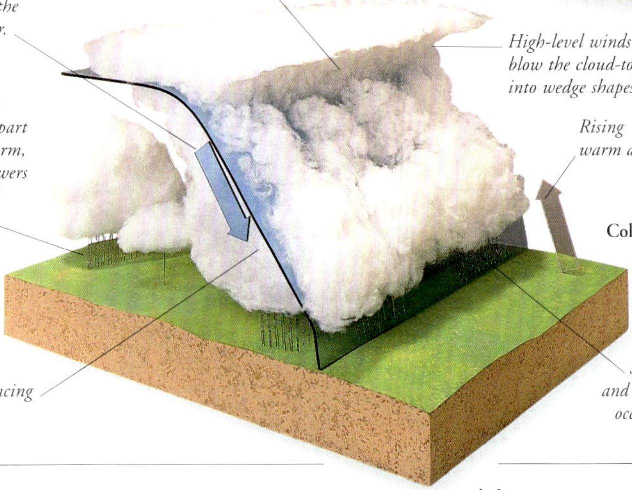

Cold front

Warm front

In a depression, the front often breaks into two – a warm front and a cold front. As the depression passes, the warm front is usually ahead of the cold. The warm air slides gently up over the cold, bringing gentle, steady rain.

Cold front

After the warm front has passed, there is generally a brief pause. The cold air then drives sharply under the warm, forcing it upwards and creating huge clouds that bring heavy rain and thunderstorms.

Formation of a depression

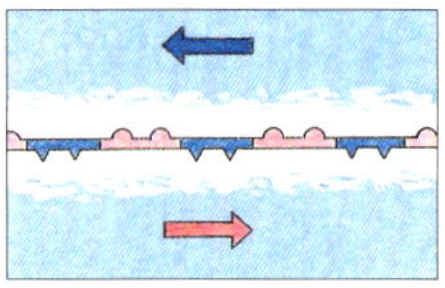

1 A polar front is where warm, tropical air meets cold, polar air.

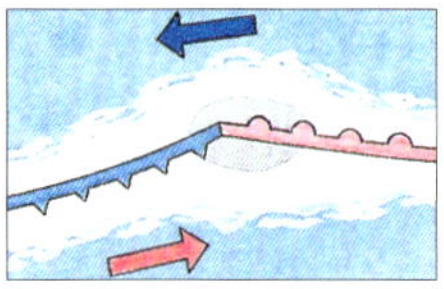

2 A depression begins to form, where warm air bulges over the cold air.

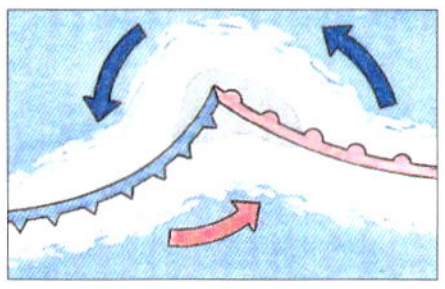

3 Cold air chases under the warm air and the front splits into two – warm and cold fronts.

4 The cold front may lift the warm front off the ground, to form an occluded front.

Air pressure

The force of molecules (groups of atoms) moving in the air creates air pressure. The more molecules are in motion, the greater the pressure. Warm air expands, making it less dense and reducing pressure. Cold air contracts, raising pressure. Pressure variations cause changes in the weather.

Barometer

Barometers measure air pressure and show changes in pressure on a dial. A dramatic fall in pressure usually means that a storm is on its way.

Aneroid barometer

Isobars

Air pressure is measured in millibars and is shown on weather maps by isobars (lines). Each isobar links points of equal pressure. The closer together the isobars are, the sharper the difference in air pressure.

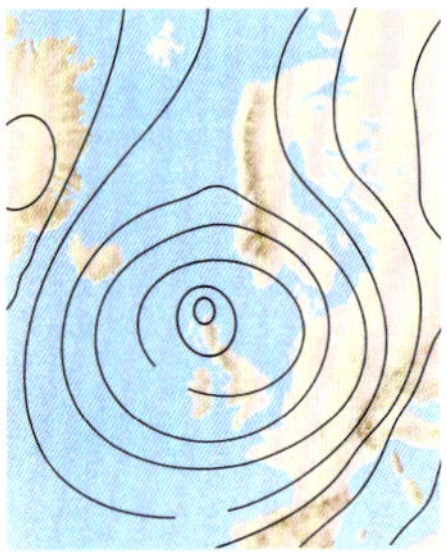

Weather map showing isobars

Air temperature

Air temperature largely depends on the Sun's heat. Air temperatures are highest in the tropics, where the Sun is strongest. Meteorologists place thermometers in the shade, when measuring air temperatures, to get an overall picture.

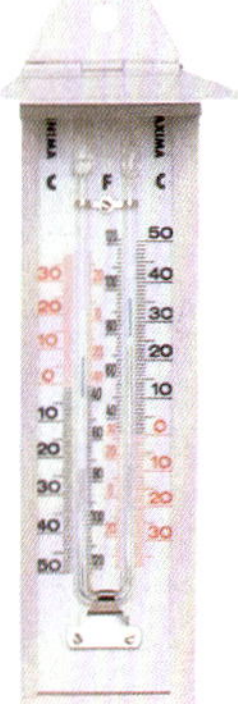

Double-ended thermometer records the daily maximum and minimum temperatures.

Humidity

Humidity is the moisture content of clouds. Moisture is present as vapour in the air almost all of the time, but is invisible. When the air gets cold, however, the vapour condenses to water drops, forming clouds, fog, or even rain.

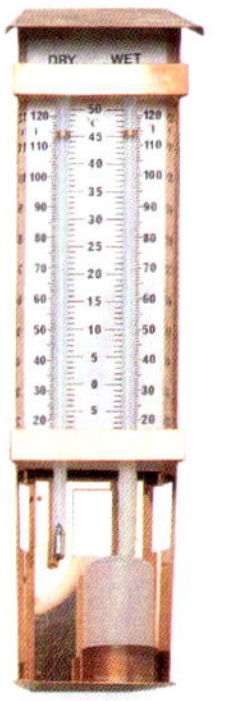

Wet and dry hygrometer uses a scale to show humidity.

FIND OUT MORE
AIR | ATMOSPHERE | CLIMATE | CLOUDS | RAIN | STORMS | TIME | WEATHER FORECASTING

WEATHER FORECASTING

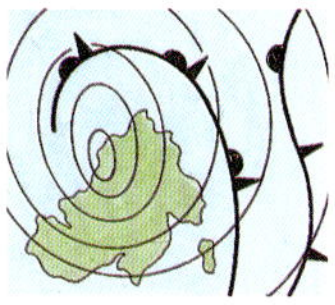

FROM FARMERS TO ICE-CREAM makers, different communities, businesses, and individuals want to know what the weather is likely to be. Weather forecasting is the prediction of weather conditions over an area, either for days (short-range) or for months (long-range). Every three hours, 10,000 weather stations world-wide simultaneously record observations of weather conditions. These data, called synoptic values, feed huge computers in the 13 main weather centres of the World Meteorological Organization. Meteorologists – people who study the weather – produce weather forecasts based on the computers' calculations plus satellite and radar images.

Weather charts

Some of the first weather forecasts were printed in the London *Daily News* in 1848. These reports were crude and very short-term compared to today's sophisticated predictions. Technology now enables satellite images of the weather to be taken from high above the Earth. A computer applies different colours to the map to indicate variations in temperature, humidity, clouds, and atmospheric pressure.

Swirl of cloud indicates a severe storm over the British Isles.

Images are taken from hundreds of miles above ground level.

Dark grey cloud shows heavy rain.

Colours show that it is generally warmer inland than on the coast.

Patchy cloud cover

Ocean is dark blue to reflect cool temperature.

Colour spectrum shows temperatures, with red denoting the hottest and violet the coolest.

Orange and red tinting indicates very hot weather.

Satellite image of Europe and North Africa taken in 1997

Lewis Richardson

British mathematician Lewis Richardson (1881–1953) devised a system called numerical forecasting. This system forecast the weather, by feeding millions of simultaneous measurements of atmospheric conditions into giant computers.

Natural weather forecasters

Natural signs are still used to help forecast the weather. Many plants and animals react to moisture changes in the air, and so may indicate that rain is coming.

Closed pine cone scales warn of rain.

Wool shrinks and curls up in dry air.

Seaweed becomes limp in moist air.

Weather stations

Ships at sea, city roofs, and mountain-tops all provide sites for the world's weather stations. Most stations are equipped with thermometers and hygrometers to show temperature and humidity, anemometers to record wind speed, rain gauges to collect rainfall, and mercury barometers to monitor changes in air pressure.

Stevenson screen
Air temperature readings are taken in the shade. A white box, called a Stevenson screen, shields thermometers from direct sunlight. Ventilation slats keep air flowing freely.

Radiosondes are filled with helium.

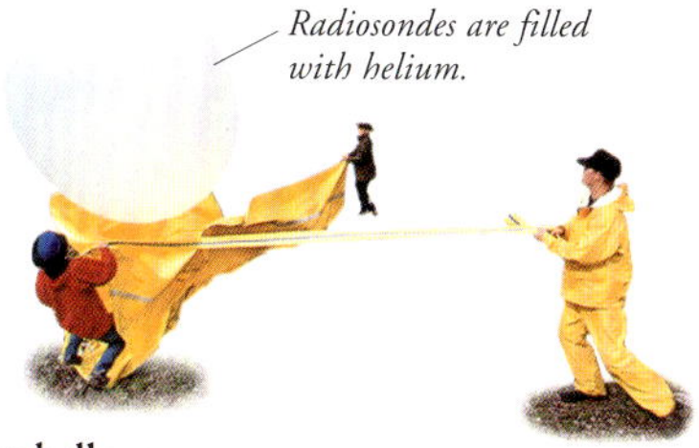

Weather balloon
Every day around the world, at noon and midnight GMT (Greenwich Mean Time), balloons, known as radiosondes, are launched into the atmosphere to measure conditions such as air pressure, temperature, and humidity at heights up to 20 km (12 miles).

Weather planes
These provide detailed information about conditions high in the atmosphere, especially around storms. Weather planes are equipped with a range of monitoring devices to record anything from the ice content of clouds to the presence of gases.

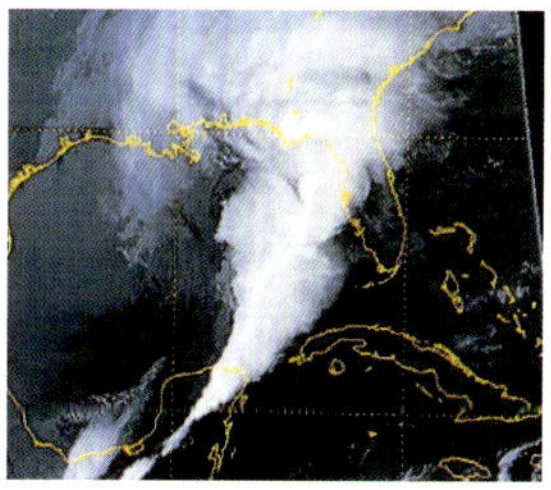

Weather satellites
The first weather satellite, launched by the USA in 1960, orbited 850 km (531 miles) above the North and South poles. In the 1970s, geostationary satellites were made to travel up to 40,000 km (25,000 miles) away.

Radar
Radar (which stands for Radio Detection And Ranging) signals reflect off water present in the air, such as snow and rain. Radar can be used to generate computer images of depressions and other systems to give a clear indication of where rain is falling, and how much.

A depression over the United Kingdom

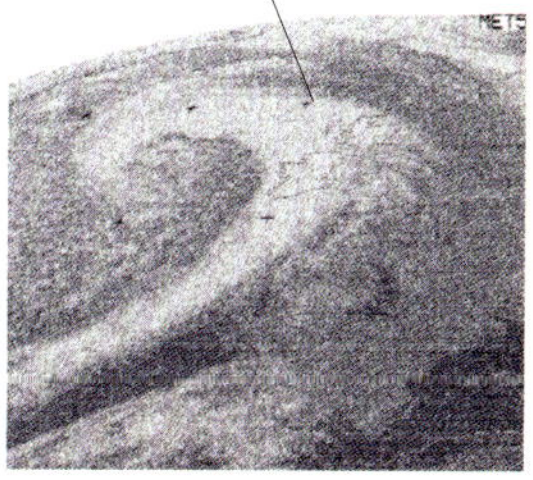

FIND OUT MORE
AIRSHIPS AND BALLOONS | ATMOSPHERE | COMPUTERS | RADAR AND SONAR | SATELLITES | TREES | WEATHER

WEIGHTS AND MEASURES

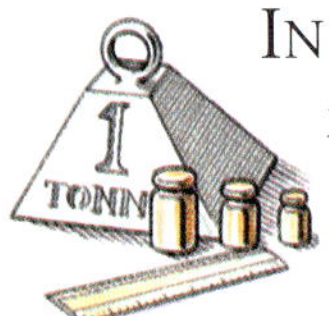

IN ANCIENT EGYPT, the cubit was the main unit used to measure length. It was based on the distance from a person's elbow to his or her fingertips. Because different people have arms of different size, it eventually became necessary for the Egyptians to define a standard length for the cubit, so that the cubit was the same throughout the country. In the same way, our modern systems of measurement, such as the metric and imperial or customary systems, are based on standard units. The quantities we measure include length, area, volume, weight, and mass.

Measuring space

When we measure length, area, or volume, we are measuring space. Length is the amount of linear space between two points. Area is a measurement of the two-dimensional space of a surface such as a wall. Volume is the amount of three-dimensional space occupied by a solid object or an amount of liquid or gas.

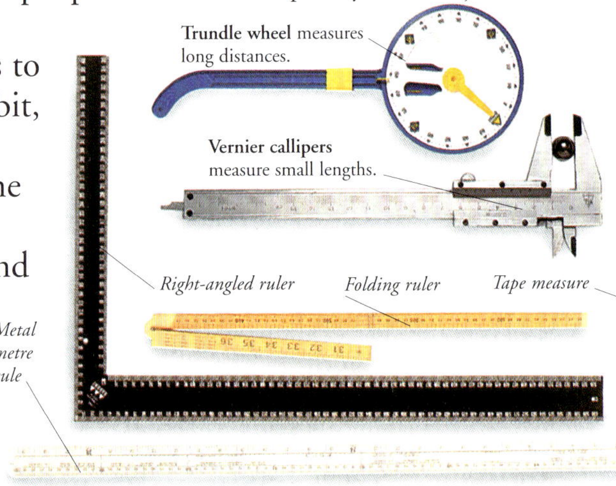

Trundle wheel measures long distances.

Vernier callipers measure small lengths.

Right-angled ruler

Folding ruler

Metal metre rule

Tape measure

Retractable steel rule

Length and distance

All devices designed to measure length or distance measure space along a line. The word length is used when measuring how long an object is; distance refers to the space between two places. Units of length or distance include the foot (ft), metre (m), mile (mi), and kilometre (km).

Measuring weight

Digital scales

We usually describe an object's "weight" in grams and kilograms, or pounds and ounces. However, these are really units of mass – that is, the amount of matter in an object. In science, weight refers to the force of gravity pulling an object downwards. Scientists measure weight in different units, such as newtons and poundals.

Scales and balances

To weigh things accurately, we must use scales or a balance. Digital scales use electronic components to find the weight of an object. A balance consists of two linked pans. The object to be weighed is placed in one pan, and standard weights are added to the other. The two pans will balance when they are carrying the same weight.

Flour

Simple balance

Weights

Area

To ensure you buy enough paint to cover a wall, it is important to know the area of the wall you are gong to paint. Area is measured in square units, such as square metres (m^2) or square feet (ft^2). Land areas are usually measured in different units, such as hectares (ha) or acres (ac).

The combined volume of the bricks equals the volume of the water.

0.64 l of water

Ten bricks, each 64 cm^3 volume

Volume

Solid volume is measured in cubic units, such as cubic centimetres (cm^3) or cubic inches (in^3). Capacity units, such as litres (l) or pints (pt), measure liquid volume. Gas volume is measured in either cubic units or capacity units.

Standard units

Today, there are two major systems of standard units. The metric system, which is decimal, is the most common and is used by scientists world-wide. Some countries, such as the USA, use the older imperial or customary system. In other countries, such as the UK, people use the metric and imperial systems side by side.

Metric system

Units in the metric system include the centimetre (cm), metre (m), gram (g), kilogram (kg), litre (l), and hectare (ha). Prefixes such as milli- and kilo- denote smaller or larger units. For example, one-thousandth of a metre is a millimetre (mm), and 1,000 metres is one kilometre (km).

Imperial system

The inch (in), foot (ft), ounce (oz), pound (lb), pint (pt), and acre (ac) are all imperial units. Unlike metric units, which are all based on the number 10, imperial units do not all have the same number base: a foot is divided into 12 inches, but a pound contains 16 ounces.

Non-standard units

Parts of the body were once used as measuring units. The hand, for example, was used to find the height of horses. Such units were non-standard, because people's bodies are never the same. A horse could be 18 hands high to one person, but only 16 to another. The hand has now been standardized to a length of exactly 10 cm (3.94 in).

Thread (length): 8 m; 26 ft

Ribbon (length): 25 cm; 10 in

Oil (volume): 1 l; 1.76 pt

Cereal (mass): 250 g; 9 oz

Flour (mass): 0.5 kg; 1.1 lb

Grapes (mass): 200 g; 7 oz

Rug (area) 6 m^2; 64 ft^2

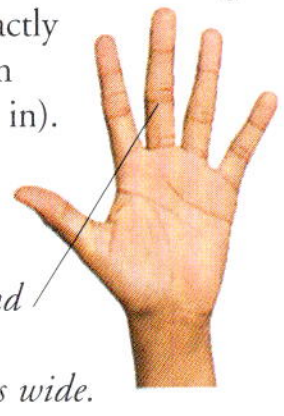

A hand was 4 fingers wide.

FIND OUT MORE
DYES AND PAINTS | EGYPT, ANCIENT | FOOD | GRAVITY | HORSES | MATHEMATICS | MATTER | NUMBERS | SCIENCE

W

WHALES AND DOLPHINS

OF ALL MARINE MAMMALS, the best adapted to life in the sea are the whales. Underneath their thick smooth skin is a layer of blubber, which insulates them against the cold. Like all mammals, they are warm-blooded, air-breathing animals, and give birth to live young. Whales, including dolphins and porpoises, form the order Cetacea, and most probably evolved from four-legged land mammals. They are separated into two groups – the toothed whales, of which there are about 80 species, and the baleen, or whalebone, whales, of which there are about 12 species. The only other entirely aquatic mammals are the Sirenians.

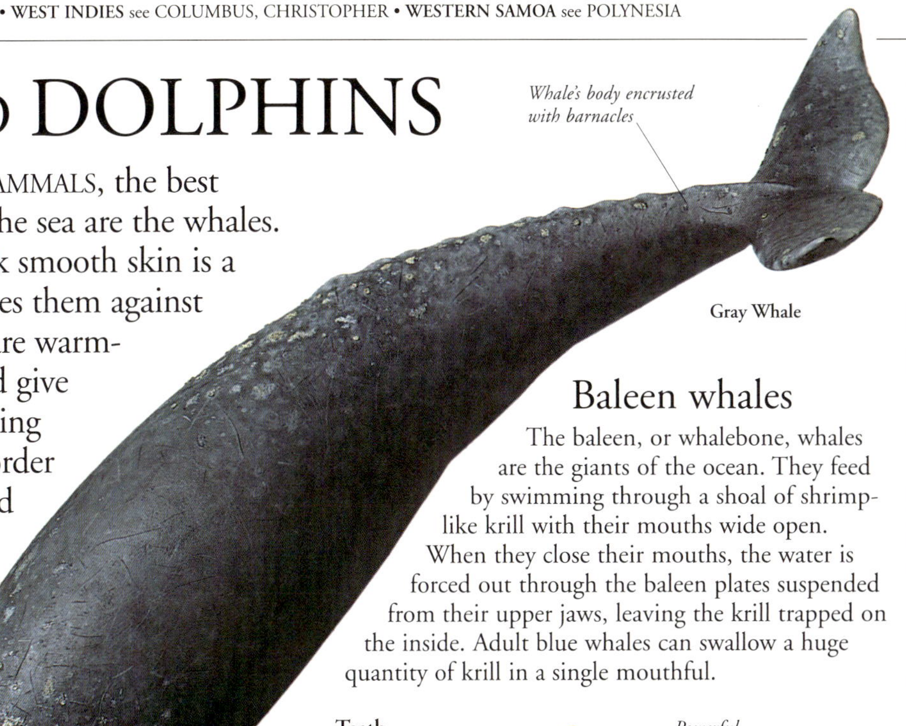

Gray Whale

Baleen whales

The baleen, or whalebone, whales are the giants of the ocean. They feed by swimming through a shoal of shrimp-like krill with their mouths wide open. When they close their mouths, the water is forced out through the baleen plates suspended from their upper jaws, leaving the krill trapped on the inside. Adult blue whales can swallow a huge quantity of krill in a single mouthful.

Gray whale
A baleen whale, the gray whale feeds on crustaceans living on the seabed. It uses its snout to stir up sediment which it strains through short baleen plates. Each year, the California gray whale migrates from its feeding grounds in the Arctic Ocean to its calving lagoons in southern California and Mexico.

Aerial view of a whale "blowing"

Blowholes
In the course of evolution, the nostrils of almost all the whales have moved to the top of the head. This makes it possible for the animals to breathe without having to expose their body above the surface of the water. Toothed whales have one blowhole; baleen whales have two. When a whale surfaces, it "spouts" by blowing moist air out through its blowhole. Then it breathes in, closes its blowhole, and submerges again.

Baleen
Plates of baleen are made from keratin. This is the same material that makes up human hair.

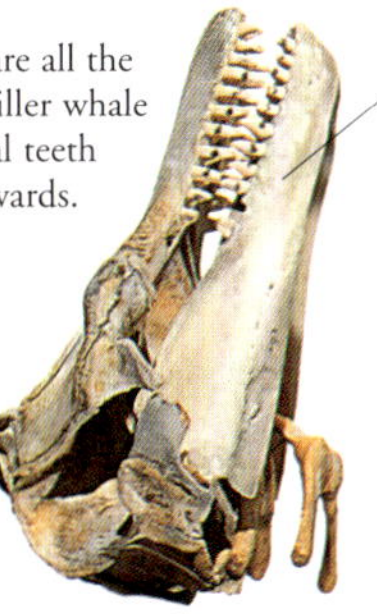

Teeth
A whale's teeth are all the same shape. A killer whale has stout, conical teeth that curve backwards.

Toothed whales

Dolphins, porpoises, sperm whales, beaked whales, and the killer whale are all species of toothed whale. The unusual narwhal and beluga also belong to this group. The toothed whales have as many as 260 teeth or as few as a single pair. The whales use their teeth to catch and hold, but not to chew, their prey which includes fish and squid. Instead, they swallow their food whole.

Killer whale
A powerful and ruthless predator, the killer whale eats mainly fish, penguins, and seals. It is particularly efficient when hunting for food as a pack. Even a large whale stands little chance against a pack of killer whales.

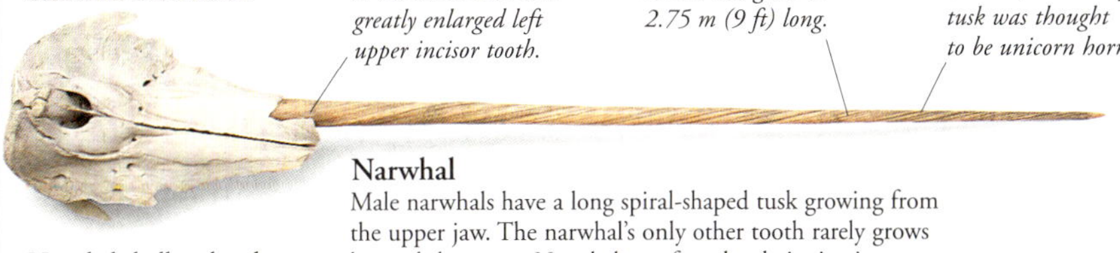

Narwhal skull and tusk

Narwhal
Male narwhals have a long spiral-shaped tusk growing from the upper jaw. The narwhal's only other tooth rarely grows beyond the gums. Narwhals are found only in Arctic waters, where they live in herds of about 12 individuals.

Common dolphin
Found in warm and temperate seas, the common dolphin sometimes gathers in schools of several hundred. It feeds on fish and is itself often caught in nets. As a result, its numbers have declined.

Porpoising
Dolphins are renowned for their ability to make spectacular leaps out of the water. This is called porpoising, but, strangely enough, porpoises do not leap.

Dolphins and porpoises

Both dolphins and porpoises are toothed whales. They eat fish, cuttlefish, and squid. Most dolphins are larger than porpoises, which have rounder bodies and foreheads.

W

Fluking
A whale's tail is horizontal and flattened. It provides the whale with its means of propulsion and generates enormous power. Before beginning a deep dive, some whales lift their tail flukes into the air to help them get into position for a steep descent. This is called fluking. The way a whale flukes helps in its identification. Some, such as this sperm whale, bring their tails high into the air so that the underside can be seen. Others keep the flukes turned down.

Threats
The great whales have few natural enemies other than the killer whale. Smaller whales are at risk from sharks. Whales are still hunted by humans, and many species are on the verge of extinction. Even dolphins and porpoises are killed. A great number of whales are caught in fishing nets and drown.

Beaching
These pilot whales have become stranded on a beach in Tasmania, Australia. No one is sure why whales do this. One theory is that they rely on the Earth's magnetic field to orientate themselves, and sometimes become confused, as, for example, during a magnetic storm. Some people think pollution of the seas weakens the whales' resistance to disease.

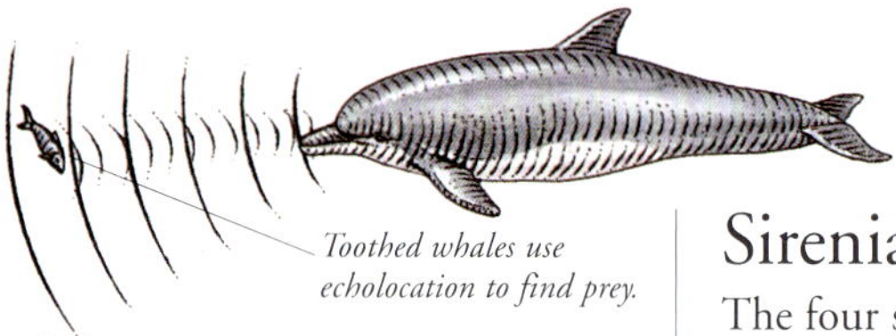

Toothed whales use echolocation to find prey.

Echolocation
Toothed whales have developed an extremely sophisticated sense of hearing. Like bats, whales use a system of echolocation to detect other things in the water. They emit an almost non-stop stream of "clicks" that cannot be detected by the human ear. The clicks are reflected off nearby objects and picked up by the whales' receiving apparatus.

Sirenians
The four species of Sirenians – three manatee and one dugong – are, like the whales, aquatic mammals. Often called sea cows, they are all herbivorous, feeding mainly on sea grasses. Manatees live in tropical coastal waters on either side of the Atlantic, entering large rivers and estuaries and rarely venturing into the open sea. The dugong lives around the edges of the Indian and western Pacific oceans.

West Indian manatee

Schools
Most whales live in communities. They associate in groups, called schools when referring to dolphins, or pods when referring to larger toothed whales such as these killer whales. The groups vary in size from a male, several females, and their calves, to thousands as sometimes happens with pilot whales.

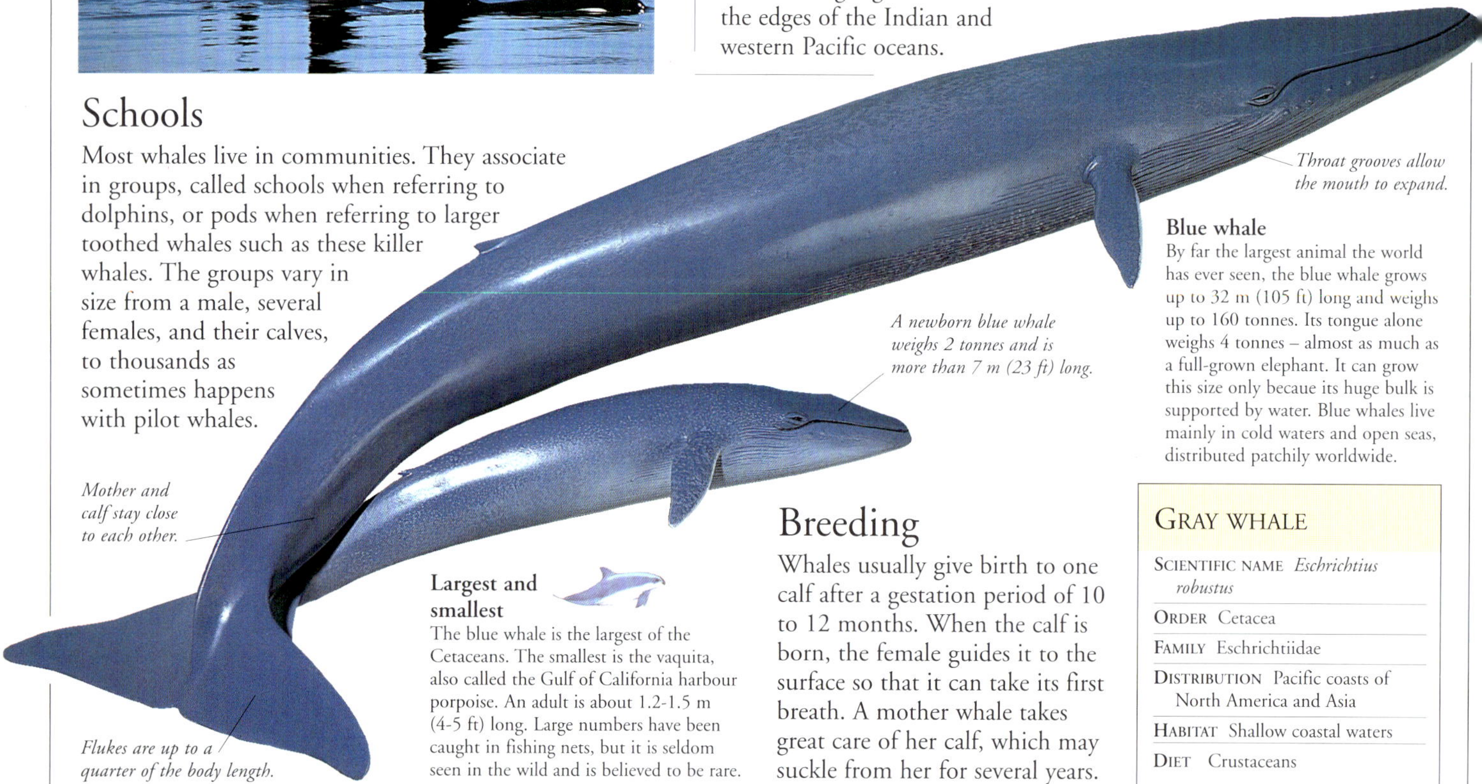

Blue whale
By far the largest animal the world has ever seen, the blue whale grows up to 32 m (105 ft) long and weighs up to 160 tonnes. Its tongue alone weighs 4 tonnes – almost as much as a full-grown elephant. It can grow this size only becaue its huge bulk is supported by water. Blue whales live mainly in cold waters and open seas, distributed patchily worldwide.

Largest and smallest

The blue whale is the largest of the Cetaceans. The smallest is the vaquita, also called the Gulf of California harbour porpoise. An adult is about 1.2-1.5 m (4-5 ft) long. Large numbers have been caught in fishing nets, but it is seldom seen in the wild and is believed to be rare.

Breeding
Whales usually give birth to one calf after a gestation period of 10 to 12 months. When the calf is born, the female guides it to the surface so that it can take its first breath. A mother whale takes great care of her calf, which may suckle from her for several years.

GRAY WHALE	
SCIENTIFIC NAME	*Eschrichtius robustus*
ORDER	Cetacea
FAMILY	Eschrichtiidae
DISTRIBUTION	Pacific coasts of North America and Asia
HABITAT	Shallow coastal waters
DIET	Crustaceans

FIND OUT MORE: BATS · MAMMALS · MIGRATION, ANIMAL · OCEAN WILDLIFE · POLAR WILDLIFE · SEALS · SHARKS AND RAYS

Whales and dolphins

Toothed

Narwhal – only the male has a long tusk, which is one of two teeth.

Head is full of an oily substance called spermaceti oil.

Sperm whale is the largest toothed whale. Males are up to 18 m (59 ft) long.

Baird's beaked whale is one of 18 species of beaked whale.

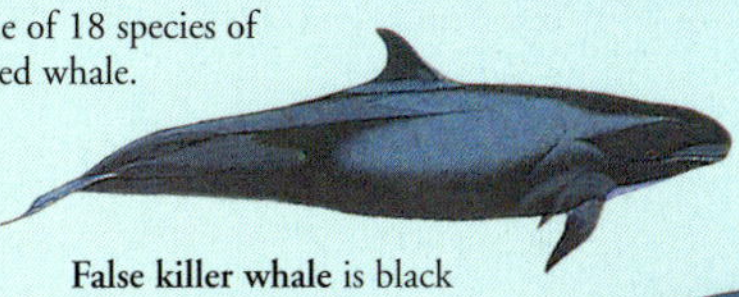

False killer whale is black all over. It is closely related to the killer whale.

Killer whale is the fastest marine mammal. It can move at up to 56 km/h (34 mph).

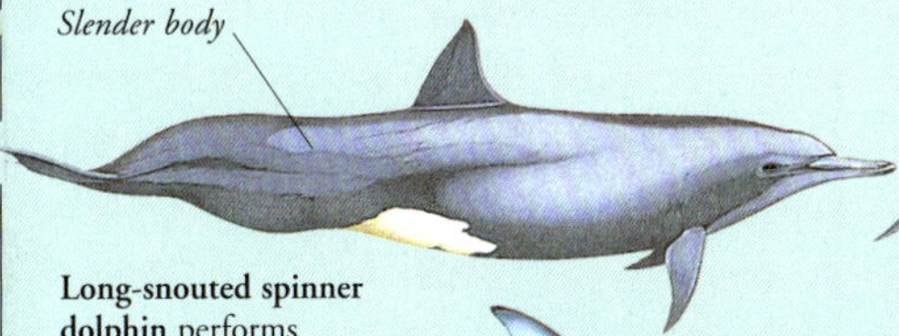

Long-snouted spinner dolphin performs spectacular aerial displays.

Hector's dolphin is one of the smallest of all cetaceans.

Amazon river dolphin is the largest of the river dolphins.

Dusky dolphin lives in groups and also likes the company of other species.

Dall's porpoise lives in deep ocean waters.

La Plata dolphin lives in the sea, preferring shallow water.

Harbour porpoise is also known as the common porpoise.

Yangtze River dolphin is also known as the baiji.

Baleen

Humpback whale is easy to recognize by its long flippers.

Pygmy right whale is the smallest baleen whale.

Right whale has a huge head, with up to 270 pairs of baleen plates.

Bowhead whale is one of the right whales.

Minke whale has a sharply pointed snout.

Blue whale is the largest animal that has ever lived. It weighs up to 160 tonnes.

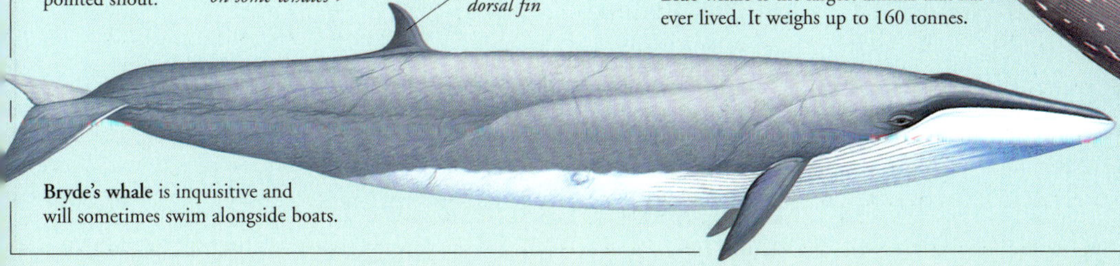

Bryde's whale is inquisitive and will sometimes swim alongside boats.

WINDS

THE AIR AROUND us is rarely still. When air moves in a continuous stream, it becomes wind. Winds are caused by air moving from areas of high pressure to areas of low pressure. Rising air does not exert great force, thereby creating an area of low pressure. Sinking air exerts more force, thereby creating an area of high pressure. Dramatic pressure differences generate strong winds, such as hurricanes. The strength of winds is measured from 0 to 12 on the Beaufort scale. Winds are part of a global circulation pattern, that keeps temperature patterns in balance.

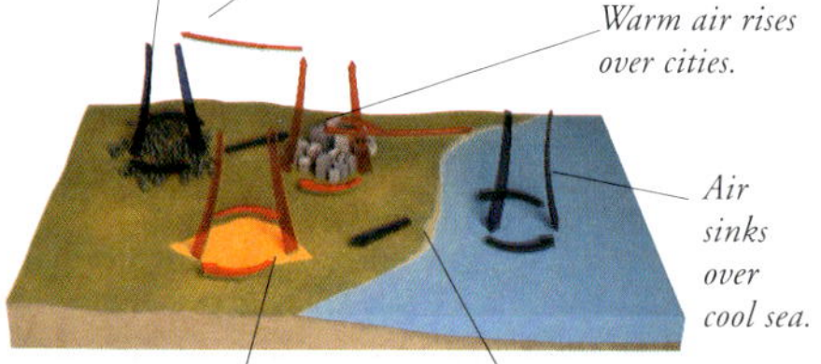

Wind generation

Low pressure areas are created where the Sun warms the Earth's surface. High pressure areas are created where the air is cooler. The extra pressure in these zones, (anticyclones, or highs) pushes air towards low pressure zones (depressions, or lows). At ground level, low-level winds blow from high to low; higher up, winds spread out above low pressure areas.

Local winds

Some winds only blow in certain places and at particular times, such as North America's Chinook. Cattlemen in the Rocky Mountains like the Chinook as this warm, dry wind rapidly removes snow cover.

Approach of strong winds

Prevailing winds

Winds are described by the direction from which they blow. A wind blowing from west to east is called a westerly, or west wind. In most places, the wind usually blows from one direction most of the time. This is known as the prevailing wind.

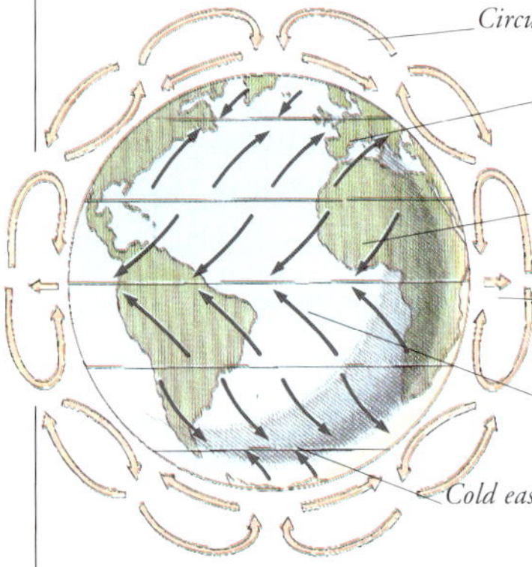

Hadley cells

Prevailing winds are the ground-level part of huge cells of circulating air. For every wind at ground level, there is a turning high-level wind. The cell in the tropics is called a Hadley cell, after English meteorologist George Hadley (1685–1768).

Coriolis effect

The Earth's rotation stops winds from blowing straight from high to low pressure areas. Instead, it deflects winds sideways. This is known as the Coriolis effect. In the northern hemisphere, winds are deflected to the right, and in the southern to the left.

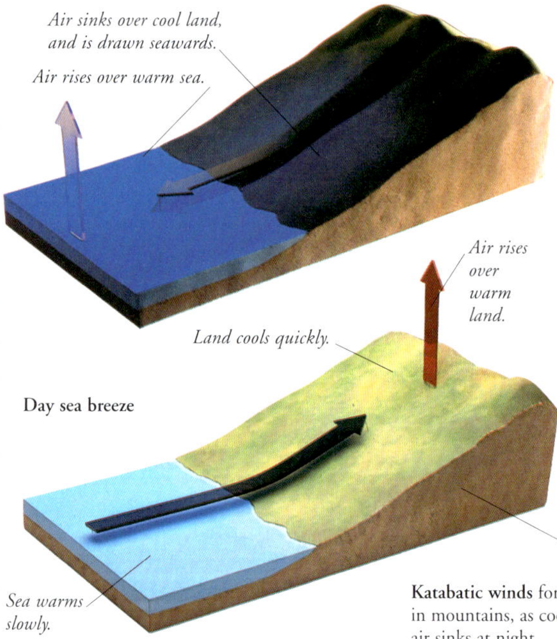

Land and sea breezes

The land heats up faster than the sea, so warm air rises over the land during the day as it is warmed by the Sun. At certain times of year, this can create a sea breeze, which is a gentle breeze blowing in to the land off the cold sea. At night, the land cools faster than the sea, reversing the air flow. This creates a land breeze, that blows out to sea.

Mountain winds

Mountains often generate their own local winds. At night, cool air flows down into valleys, creating katabatic winds. In the day, sun-warmed air rises out of the valleys, creating anabatic winds.

Katabatic winds form in mountains, as cool air sinks at night.

Anabatic winds form in valleys, as warm air rises during the day.

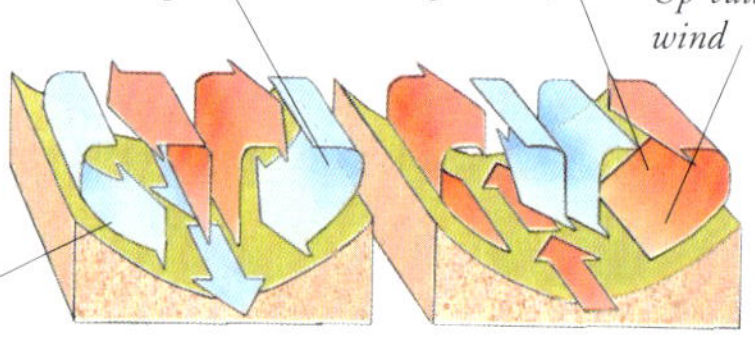

Jet streams

At high altitudes, there are narrow rivers of air that roar steadily around the world at speeds of 370 kmh (230 mph) or more. This photograph shows a jet stream high over the Sahara in Egypt.

Rossby wave

Between the westerly winds and the polar easterlies, a jet stream runs eastwards. It meanders around the world in four to six giant waves, called Rossby waves, that form cyclonic storms below.

1 A Rossby wave develops as a major bend forms in the polar front of the stream.

2 The Coriolis effect makes the wave deeper and more pronounced.

3 Caught in the loops, warm and cold air may detach to form cyclones.

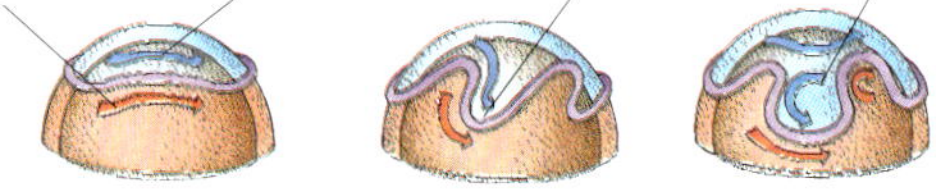

FIND OUT MORE
AIR | ATMOSPHERE | COASTS | ENERGY | KITES | MOUNTAINS AND VALLEYS | OCEANS AND SEAS | SAILING AND OTHER WATERSPORTS | SHIPS AND BOATS | WEATHER

WINTER SPORTS

THE TERM WINTER SPORTS refers to sports that take place on snow and ice. Keen competition has grown up around them, and the Winter Olympics are held every four years. There are two main types of skiing: Alpine skiing, which features downhill and slalom racing; and Nordic skiing, which is a cross-country sport that also includes ski jumping. A new type of skiing, freestyle, is about performance rather than speed. In sled racing, riders hurtle down special runs. Skating includes figures, ice hockey, and racing.

Mittens

Ski poles

Skis

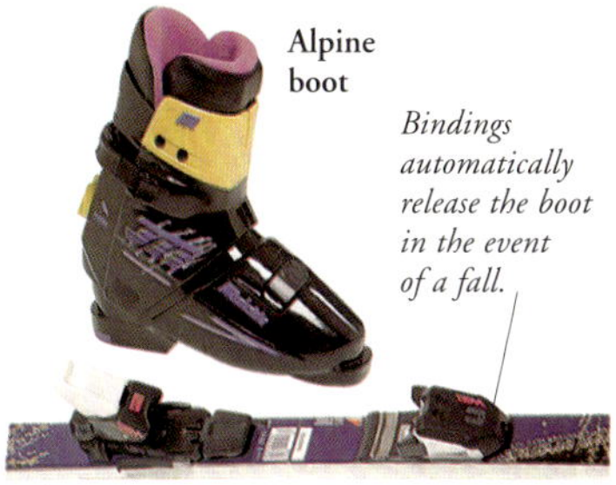

Alpine boot

Bindings automatically release the boot in the event of a fall.

Ski bindings

Skiing

Alpine racing is about speed and technique; Nordic more about stamina. The two disciplines use different equipment. Alpine skis are wider and heavier than Nordic skis, and the boots are attached to the skis with safety bindings. Nordic boots are like trainers, and the heel lifts free with each stride.

Ski jumping
In ski jumping, competitors take off from the end of a chute on a ski tower. They aim to fly gracefully, perfectly balanced and still in the air, before landing smoothly. Judges award points for style as well as distance jumped.

Nordic racing
Cross-country courses have no steep slopes or sharp turns. Races range from 5 to 50 km (3 to 30 miles), with skiers starting at 30-second intervals. Placings are decided on time. There are relays, combined events, and the biathlon, which includes shooting at targets.

Downhill racer

Alpine racing
In downhill racing, skiers take the fastest line down a set route, taking off into the air where necessary. In slaloms, skiers weave in and out of pairs of flags, or "gates". Both are decided on time.

Sled racing

Any snowy slope is a site for sled racing, but for major competitions, special steep, twisty runs are made from ice and snow. The art is to shift the bodyweight to make the sled go the fastest way down, letting gravity do the work. Riders go one at a a time, and the winner is the one with the lowest total time from up to four runs.

Luge
The luge is a one- or two-person toboggan with no brakes or steering. The riders, or sliders, use their legs and shoulders to guide the vehicle. The luge is ridden face up, in a sitting or lying position.

Toboggan
The skeleton toboggan is so-called because it has no structure above the runners. The rider lies face down, uses toe pieces for braking, and steers by shifting weight. The only major competitions are on the Cresta Run at St Moritz in Switzerland.

Bobsleigh
Two- or four-man bobs have metal runners, steering, and brakes. In a four, the two middle men help to guide the bob by shifting their weight on turns. A brake man uses the brakes only for correcting skids or for stopping.

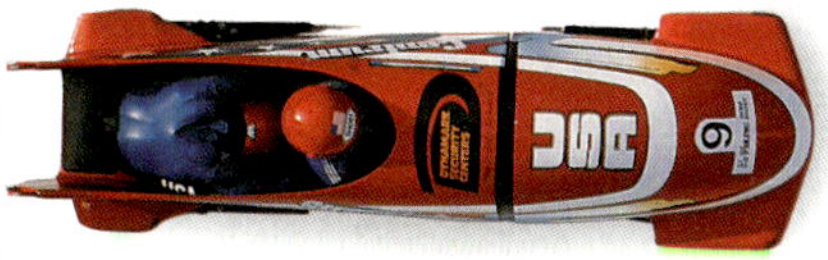

Skating

Figure skating takes place on an indoor ice rink. There are four events – men's and women's singles, mixed pairs, and ice dancing. Long-track speed skating usually takes place outdoors, and skaters race against the clock. Short-track is held indoors, with elimination heats. Ice hockey, on indoor ice rinks, is a major sport in North America and parts of Europe.

Speed skating
Long-track racing is held on a 400-m (436-yd) track with two skaters in separate lanes. There are no lanes in short-track racing, and four to six skaters jockey for position around a tight oval track.

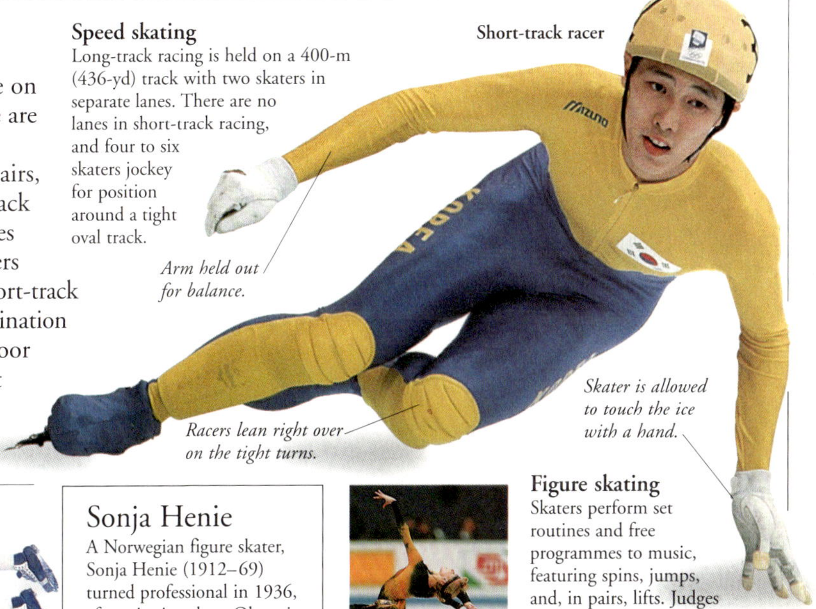

Short-track racer

Arm held out for balance.

Racers lean right over on the tight turns.

Skater is allowed to touch the ice with a hand.

Sonja Henie

A Norwegian figure skater, Sonja Henie (1912–69) turned professional in 1936, after winning three Olympic gold medals and 10 world championships. With her theatrical performances and short skirts, she revolutionized the sport. She toured the USA with her own ice show, became an American citizen, and made several films.

Figure skating
Skaters perform set routines and free programmes to music, featuring spins, jumps, and, in pairs, lifts. Judges award marks out of six for artistic impression and for technical merit. Ice dancing is less athletic, with more emphasis placed on interpretation of the music.

Referee drops the puck to restart the game.

Ice hockey
Ice hockey is played six-a-side with substitutes allowed at any time. The object is to propel a hard disc, the puck, into the opposition's goal. There are three 20-minute periods. Players serve time penalties for foul play.

FIND OUT MORE
BALL GAMES
HEALTH AND FITNESS
MOTOR SPORTS
OLYMPIC GAMES
SPORT

WITCHES AND WITCHCRAFT

THE BELIEF IN WITCHES – people with supernatural powers – is ancient and universal. No one knows whether witches do actually have special powers, but from the earliest times, people in all cultures have believed that some men and women can use rituals, spells, and other magical means to influence events for good or evil. Definitions of witchcraft vary, but it is always associated with magic. Uniquely, however, in Europe from the 15th to the 18th centuries, witchcraft was associated with devil worship, and was punishable by death.

Healing

Witchcraft has always been linked with natural religions and healing. The word "witch" comes from the Anglo-Saxon, *wicca,* meaning wise one; in medieval Europe, many so-called witches were actually village wise women, skilled in herbal cures. Today, in many Latin American and African societies, witch doctors and shamans use herbs and rituals for healing.

Foxglove

St John's Wort

Magic

Carving of African shaman

Magic, or sorcery, is the attempt to use supernatural or natural forces to influence events. Belief in magic has a long history – evidence of magic spells has been found in prehistoric cave paintings – and continues today in many cultures, as a superstition or as a religion. In some cultures, magic is considered to be sacred and is practised by specially skilled people.

Familiars

Identifying witches was difficult, because they looked exactly the same as any member of society. However, medieval people believed that true witches could fly – usually on a broomstick – and were accompanied by a "familiar", such as a cat, which was really a demon in disguise.

Torture

Suspected witches were savagely tortured in order to make them confess and also to name accomplices. Methods of torture included whipping, branding with red-hot irons, stretching on the rack, thumbscrews, and the gouging out of eyes. Most people confessed to almost anything just to stop the torture.

Eye gouger

Thumbscrews

European witch hunts

In early medieval Europe, belief in witches was a natural part of everyday life. However, from the 12th century, the Christian church redefined witchcraft as heresy, or treason against God. Witches were described as evil devil-worshippers, and the Church set up massive witch hunts in which anyone suspected of witchcraft was rounded up, tried, and often executed. The witch hunts lasted some 300 years, and at least 300,000 innocent people, mostly women, were put to death. Historians have put forward various reasons for the witch hunts. These included a general persecution of women, and the rise of medical science.

Witch trials

Persecution of supposed witches reached its height between 1580 and 1660, when trials occurred throughout western Europe. As hysteria mounted, thousands were brought before Church and civil courts. Anyone old, alone, or eccentric could be accused, including elderly women, village midwives, and herbalists. Their persecution was fuelled by gossip and rumours, which were used as evidence in court.

Witch burning

Proving witchcraft was a difficult matter, and various tests were devised. One of these was throwing a bound person into water. If she was guilty, she floated; if innocent, she sank. Death was the usual penalty for witchcraft, particularly burning at the stake, on the grounds that this punishment mirrored the fires of hell. Many thousands were put to death this way, including Joan of Arc, the French heroine who was accused of being a witch by the English and burned at the stake in 1431.

MALLEVS MALEFICARVM,
MALEFICAS ET EARVM
hæresim frameâ conterens,
EX VARIIS AVCTORIBVS COMPILATVS,
& in quatuor Tomos iustè distributus,
TOMVS PRIMVS.
LVGDVNI,
Sumptibus CLAVDII BOVRGEAT, sub signo Mercurij Galli.
M. DC. LXIX.
CVM PRIVILEGIO REGIS.

Malleus Maleficarum

In 1486, two Dominican monks, Heinrich Krämer and Jacob Sprenger, published the *Malleus Maleficarum* (Hammer of the Witches). This book included the pope's definition of witches as "anti-Christian", and set out rules for identifying, prosecuting, and punishing witches. The book quickly spread throughout Europe, and was used as the essential witch-hunter's reference.

Salem trials

The earliest English settlers took their fear of witches to the American colonies. In 1692, a series of notorious witch trials took place in Salem, Massachusetts. In all, 27 people were tried and convicted; of these, 19 were hanged, and one man was pressed to death with stones. The trials were later condemned, and the convictions overturned.

Halloween

Originally a Celtic festival for the dead, Halloween falls on 31 October. It was once believed that on this night, witches and warlocks flew abroad, and bonfires were lit to keep spirits away. Trick-or-treating has replaced witches' pranks today.

FIND OUT MORE
CRIME AND PUNISHMENT
EUROPE, HISTORY OF
HUNDRED YEARS WAR
MEDICINE, HISTORY OF
RELIGIONS

WOLVES AND WILD DOGS

THE FAMILY CANIDAE, the dog family, contains about 34 species, which can be divided into three main groups. The lupine (meaning wolf-like) group contains wolves, jackals, the coyote, wild dogs, and domestic dogs, many of which hunt in packs. The second group contains the vulpine (meaning fox-like) foxes. The third group contains the south American foxes, or zorros. Canids are mainly carnivorous. Alert, hardy mammals, they are able to catch and kill animals as large as, or larger than, themselves. They can travel long distances without tiring, keeping up a steady trot on long legs and large paws.

Foxes are lightly built for better agility.

The fox catches a small animal by pouncing on it like a cat and pinning it to the ground with its front paws.

Foxes

There are about nine species of vulpine fox, of which the red fox is the largest and most widespread. This agile animal owes its success to its intelligence and adaptability. It is able to thrive equally well in towns and in rural areas. Foxes do not form packs, but live alone or in small family groups.

Wolves

There are two species of wolf – the grey wolf and the red wolf. The red wolf is an endangered species and the grey wolf is nearly extinct in much of its former range. Wolves are social animals that live in packs led by a top male and female. The pack mark the boundary of their territory with urine and howl to tell other packs they are there.

Thick short underfur and long outer "guard" hairs insulate the wolf against freezing temperatures.

The wolf has excellent hearing, eyesight, and sense of smell.

Wolves have pale underparts, with darker fur on the body, ears, and tail to match their habitat.

Long legs with four toes on the hind feet and five on the front feet.

Most of the adults in a pack go on hunting trips.

In the snow, each wolf walks in the leader's tracks.

Raccoon dog with a white coat

Member of the fox species

Wild dogs

The African wild dog, the dhole, and the dingo are known as wild dogs, often hunting in packs over huge areas. The maned wolf, the bush dog, and the raccoon dog are distantly related canids. The raccoon dog is a timid, solitary creature that lives in dense undergrowth feeding on fruit, insects, and small animals. It stays underground in harsh winter weather.

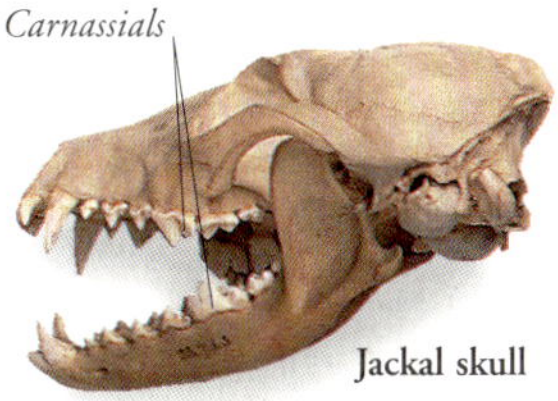

Carnassials

Jackal skull

Jackals form pairs for life.

Jackals

The four species of jackal are closely related to wolves. As with most canids, they have two sharp carnassial teeth used for cutting meat. These are situated where the jaws exert greatest force. Their long pointed canine teeth are for gripping and killing prey.

Mottled coloration gives African hunting dogs an effective camouflage.

Hunting

The most specialized pack hunters are the African hunting dogs. They hunt as an organized team, but they often lose a kill to stronger predators. Human persecution and introduced diseases have reduced their numbers drastically.

Red fox cubs do not forage with the adults until they are about 12 weeks old.

Learning skills

Cubs will not survive into adulthood unless they learn to kill and defend themselves. They learn these skills through playing, chasing, and pouncing upon each other. Social canids may learn hunting skills from the adults in their pack.

RED FOX

SCIENTIFIC NAME	*Vulpes vulpes*
ORDER	Carnivora
FAMILY	Canidae
DISTRIBUTION	North America, Eurasia, North Africa, Australia
HABITAT	Everywhere except deserts
DIET	Meat, insects, and fruit
SIZE	Length: about 110 cm (42 in)
LIFESPAN	3 years in wild

FIND OUT MORE
ANIMAL BEHAVIOUR · AFRICAN WILDLIFE · DESERT WILDLIFE · DOGS · HYENAS · MAMMALS · POLAR WILDLIFE · URBAN WILDLIFE

Wolves and wild dogs

Bush dog is a strong swimmer and hunts other aquatic animals.

An adult wolf needs to eat up to 6 kg (13 lb) of food every day.

Grey wolf is the largest wild dog. Although once widespread, it is now extinct or nearly extinct in many parts of its range.

Golden jackal shares parental duties with its mate.

Raccoon dog has a varied diet, and has large cheek teeth for grinding up fruits and seeds.

A maned wolf is about 80 cm (31 in) tall.

Maned wolf needs a large grassland territory. It lives in eastern South America.

African hunting dog has a pattern of brown, dun, and white on its body, with a white-tipped tail.

Dingo is a wild dog from Australia. It was probably introduced there about 7,000 years ago.

Rounded ears

Indian dhole has a coat that ranges from sandy brown to orange-red.

Fennec fox is the smallest member of the family.

Large ears can pick up the sounds of insects.

Bat-eared fox feeds on beetles and other invertebrates.

Ruppell's sand fox lives in North Africa and the Middle East.

Like all dogs, foxes have an acute sense of smell.

Red fox has adapted to live in suburbs and towns.

Erect ears help the fox tell from which direction a sound is coming.

Grey fox is a good climber and will make its den in large trees up to 9 m (30 ft) above the ground.

Paws are well furred to save heat.

Arctic fox has a pale winter coat and a dark summer coat.

WOMEN'S MOVEMENT

FOR THE LAST 200 YEARS, women have fought for their rights. Their struggle is sometimes called the women's movement, although the term includes different campaigns. The first wave of organized feminism – the fight for women's rights – appeared during the 1800s, and was concerned with legal rights, and the right to vote. During the 1960s, a new wave of protest – the women's liberation movement – appeared that made women's rights a global issue. By the 1990s, the women's movement had gained many victories and changed society.

Early stirrings

In the 18th century, women had no rights – they were the property of their husbands or fathers. Inspired by the French Revolution, women began to challenge this situation.

Mary Wollstonecraft

In 1792 an Englishwoman, Mary Wollstonecraft (1759–97), wrote *Vindication of the Rights of Women.* She deplored the fact that married women were kept at home "confined in cages, like the feathered race", and called for an end to their oppression.

Mary Wollstonecraft

First Wave

During the 1800s, middle-class women, such as Madame Bodichon (formerly Barbara Leigh Smith) campaigned for a married woman's right to keep her own property, and for the right to education and meaningful work.

Madame Bodichon (1827–90)

Votes for Women poster

Fight for the vote

From the 1840s, American and British women focused on fighting for the vote, because they believed that only by voting could they improve their situation. The Cause, as it became known, was a long struggle involving hundreds of thousands of women.

National Union of Women's Suffrage Societies (NUWSS) banner

Women's liberation movement

In the late 1960s, the women's liberation movement exploded on to the political scene. Increasing numbers of women around the world challenged oppression and traditional female roles. They demanded an end to all forms of sexual discrimination, and campaigned around issues such as equal pay, job opportunities, healthcare, childcare, abortion, sexuality, violence towards women, and racism.

Miss World contest, 1970

Women on strike, 1977

Equal rights

During the 1970s, the women's liberation movement was a major political influence in many countries. It forced the introduction of legislation that ensured equal rights for women by banning sex discrimination at work and in education. However, though this legislation established women's rights to equal opportunities, inequalities still existed.

Demonstrations

In 1970, feminists demonstrated at the Miss World beauty contest, protesting that it degraded women. The contest continued on a stage covered in flour and other debris thrown by the protesters. After this event, which was televised worldwide, more women began to meet in groups to discuss how sexism affected their lives, and to plan changes.

International Women's Day

In 1908, socialists in the USA set aside one day for women's suffrage demonstrations. In the 1970s, feminists revived the idea, and today women worldwide celebrate 8 March.

Silver wattle, the Women's Day emblem

Timeline

1830s Anti-slavery campaign stimulates growth of women's movement, USA.

1848 First-ever women's rights convention, Seneca Falls, USA.

1869 Susan B Anthony and Elizabeth Cady Stanton form National Woman Suffrage Association, USA.

WSPU enamel badge

1893 New Zealand women are the first to gain the vote.

1968 Women workers at Ford, UK, strike for equal pay.

1970 Australian Germaine Greer writes *The Female Eunuch;* it calls for women's liberation.

1975 Equal rights laws passed, UK.

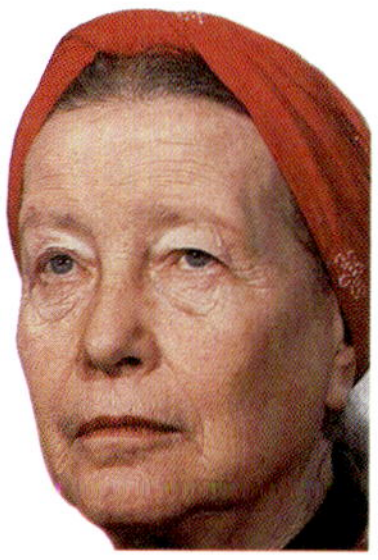

Simone de Beauvoir

French philosopher, Simone de Beauvoir (1908–86), was a major figure in modern feminism. In 1949, she wrote *Le Deuxième Sexe (The Second Sex),* in which she drew on history, art, literature, and psychology to show how men had consistently denied women's identity. Her book was very influential, and de Beauvoir herself campaigned actively for women's rights.

FIND OUT MORE
FRENCH REVOLUTION
HISTORY
HUMAN RIGHTS
PANKHURST FAMILY
TRUTH, SOJOURNER

WOODLAND WILDLIFE

IN TEMPERATE REGIONS, wherever rain often falls, woodland is the natural form of vegetation. In some areas, just a single species of tree occurs. Elsewhere, there is a mixture of needle-leaved conifers, broad-leaved trees, evergreens that keep their leaves all year, and deciduous trees that shed leaves in winter. Some woods are quite open to the sky; in others, tree crowns mingle to create a closed canopy. All woodlands are rich habitats for wildlife – there are few large animals, such as boars, but there are insects galore, and the birds that feed on them fill the habitat with their song.

Layers of the woodland

Woods are usually described as having five layers, each with its own characteristic vegetation and wildlife. A natural woodland, therefore, offers a rich mix of living spaces for wildlife, both across the habitat within clearings and streams, and in the layers that exist from the treetops down to the ground.

Canopy

Shrub layer

Field layer

Leaf litter

Canopy

The canopy consists of the crowns of the tallest trees. Branches and twigs sprout a luxuriant layer of greenery that traps most of the incoming sunlight. Here, well above ground level, the canopy provides protection from most predators for insects, birds, and tree-climbing mammals, such as squirrels.

Shrub layer

Beneath the canopy grow woody plants, including shrubs and bushes that never reach great height, such as hazel and hawthorn, and young trees yet to grow to maturity. They form an often densely foliaged layer, which provides nest sites for birds and plentiful insect food.

Field layer

Wildflowers, ferns, mosses, and other low-growing vegetation grow on the ground and are called the field layer. They can tolerate shade because so much sunlight is trapped by the trees above. These plants provide food for insects and snails and cover for small animals, such as rodents and weasels.

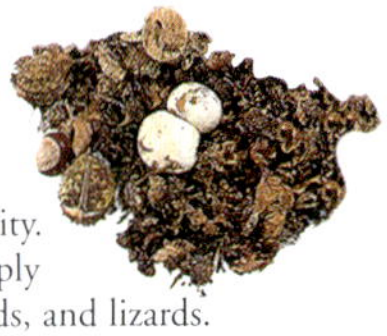

Leaf litter

The slow decay of fallen leaves creates a layer of leaf litter on the ground. Mixed with fallen twigs, nuts, and berries, the litter harbours its own wildlife community. Millipedes and beetles live here and supply food for foraging mammals, ground birds, and lizards.

Soil

Plants take root in soil that is richly supplied with nutrients from decaying leaf litter above. Moles tunnel through soil, and other mammals make their burrows here. Soil also provides food for beetle larvae and earthworms.

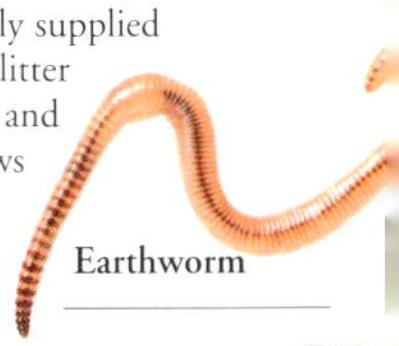

Earthworm

Mammals

Seldom seen because of their secretive or nocturnal habits, woodland mammals betray their presence in various ways – in the rustle of leaves made by a mouse in the undergrowth, in the fresh earth around the entrance to a fox's burrow, or in a track of hoof prints made by deer across fresh snow. Many mammals forage or hunt on the woodland floor; others climb into the trees to find food and shelter.

Chipmunk feeding

Eastern chipmunk

This chipmunk from North America moves easily through the layers of a woodland. It climbs among the branches, forages for seeds and nuts on the woodland floor, and makes its home in a burrow in the soil.

Roe deer

Foliage from the field layer up to the lower shrub layer provides food for the shy roe deer, which lives either alone or in small groups. Unable to climb or burrow, deer rely on their keen senses, inconspicuous colouring, and speed to avoid danger. When alarmed, the white hairs on the roe deer's rump fluff out.

Roe deer within deep foliage

Badger at entrance to burrow

European badger

Extensive family burrows, or "setts", dug out with strong claws, are the hallmark of European badgers. Each sett has a series of underground chambers, a network of tunnels, and several entrances from the woodland floor. Badgers emerge at night to rifle through leaf litter in search of worms, grubs, fruit, and nuts.

Birds

Woodland birdlife is wonderfully diverse. There are ground foragers, such as pheasants, berry-eaters of the shrub layer, such as blackbirds, songsters in the treetops, and menacing birds of prey that twist and turn among the branches as they swoop for the kill. Summer is the busiest time; when autumn comes, leaves fall, woodland life is at a low ebb, and many birds migrate to warmer climates far away.

Green woodpecker

Woodpeckers are famous for hammering rapidly into tree trunks with their sharp beaks to excavate nests. The green woodpecker climbs trunks to dig insect larvae out of the bark, but it also forages on the ground where it breaks into ants' nests to feast on the occupants.

Dappled brown feathers help conceal the owl by day.

Tawny owl

The tawny owl hunts at night. It rests in the canopy and scans the ground for prey – its huge eyes and sensitive ears alert for the slightest movement from a shrew or rodent. Then, with a silent, agile swoop, the owl pounces on its victim.

Common nightjar

The common nightjar visits temperate woodlands to breed in summer, but migrates to Africa in winter. It lives at the edge of forests, and in more open woods where it darts through the air at night chasing moths. By day, it rests on branches or on the ground, camouflaged by its mottled plumage.

Well-camouflaged nightjar

Reptiles

Most woodlands are inhabited by lizards and snakes. Many of them make their home on the ground, among the leaf litter beneath logs and rocks, or in hollow tree trunks; others climb into the shrubs above to hunt for insects and birds. The world's most northern woods are too cold for all but a few species of reptile that spend the winter in hibernation.

Anole lizard

With their long toe pads for gripping branches, anoles are among the most adept tree-climbers of all lizards. The green anole of North America hunts for insects and spiders among foliage, where its body colour provides effective camouflage. When the lizard scurries down a trunk or crosses the woodland floor, however, it changes to a brown colour within seconds.

Rat snake

Living in the woodlands of North America, the rat snake preys on small mammals, birds, and lizards. In many areas, the cold winter weather forces the snake into hibernation. Concealing itself deep in leaf litter or in a hollow log, the snake enters a state of dormancy that can last several months.

Amphibians

Although amphibians usually live in or near water, many species find the humid conditions they need in woodlands – both near streams and in the cool shade beneath a mature canopy. Toads and salamanders spend much of their lives crawling through damp leaf litter and undergrowth, snatching invertebrates to feed on. A few species of frog are adapted for foraging up into the trees themselves.

North American tree frog

Tree frogs live in warmer areas of woodland across the world, where they snap up insects and spiders among the leaves of trees. They have loose belly skin and sucker-like toe discs enabling them to climb vertical surfaces. Tree frogs camouflage themselves by changing their skin colour to match their surroundings.

Spotted salamander

Salamanders are numerous in the damp mountain woods of the eastern USA. The spotted salamander spends most of its time hidden within leaf litter and soil, hunting for invertebrates such as worms and slugs. Instead of being camouflaged, it is brightly coloured which acts as a warning to any predator that it is poisonous to eat.

Insects

During spring, when eggs have hatched and any overwintering larvae or adults have emerged from dormancy, a woodland is alive with insects. From the sunlit canopy to the perpetual darkness of the soil layer, insects are busy gathering nectar, hunting each other, munching leaves and wood, and processing debris.

Wood ant

Wood ants live in huge colonies on the ground where they build domed nests of twigs and leaves, or pine needles. The queen ant produces batch after batch of young, while worker ants go out in search of food for the colony.

Cardinal beetle

The grubs of this brightly coloured beetle are among many beetle larvae that bore their way under tree bark. Here they remain safe from most predators, but they may still be plucked from hiding by woodpeckers.

Tree wasp

Tree wasps live in large colonies. They make nests of paper-like material that they suspend from the branches of trees and shrubs. Workers make the paper by scraping off and chewing fragments of wood from trees with their strong jaws, and mixing it with saliva.

Stag beetle

The stag beetle lays its eggs in rotting wood on the woodland floor. Male stag beetles use their impressive jaws not for feeding, but to brandish at rival males. During a fight, two rivals use their jaws like antlers to grapple and wrestle with one another. Stag beetles are the largest British beetle and may reach 7 cm (2.8 in) in length.

Old lady moth

Adults of the old lady moth appear only in high summer, flying at night, but hiding during the day in hollow trees. The larvae, or caterpillars, relish the leaves of some woodland shrubs. The larvae live longer than the adults, first emerging from eggs in late summer and spending the winter in hibernation.

Plants and fungi

Tall trees dominate woodlands, but many other types of vegetation exist with them, such as shrubs, creepers, mosses, and ferns. Wildflowers often bloom early in spring, taking advantage of the light available before new leaves on trees have grown. Most of these plants are adapted to grow in shade, and can extract the energy they need for growth from the sunlight that filters down to their leaves. Fungi and some orchids do not need light but obtain their energy directly from other plants.

Oak galls

Galls are abnormal growths caused by gall wasps, which lay their eggs in the leaves of oak trees. When the grubs hatch, they cause the plant tissue to grow in a protective, food-rich ball around them.

Bracket fungus

Many types of fungi live near the shady woodland floor. Bracket fungus often sprouts from old tree trunks. Using fine root-like structures, fungi draw energy and nutrients from the plant matter on which they grow.

Pine cone

The needle leaves of pine trees offer little sustenance to animals, but their seed cones are full of nutritious food for many creatures. Squirrels and jays break into new cones to extract the seeds, while other animals wait for the cones to open and shed their contents.

Ferns

Ferns are simple plants that produce spores instead of flowers. They are common in the humid shade of woodlands, where carpets of ferns can dominate the field layer. In warm climates, ferns grow so big that they form part of the shrub layer.

FIND OUT MORE
AMPHIBIANS · BEETLES · CAMOUFLAGE AND COLOUR · FORESTS · HIBERNATION · INSECTS · MUSHROOMS AND OTHER FUNGI · PLANTS · REPTILES · SOIL · TREES

WOODPECKERS AND TOUCANS

THEY LOOK DIFFERENT, and also feed in different ways, yet woodpeckers and toucans are close relatives. They live in forests and woodlands, and most of them spend nearly all their time in trees, making their nests in holes in the trunks. Woodpeckers usually feed by chiselling their way into wood to reach burrowing insects. Toucans clamber about among the treetops and use their huge colourful beaks to collect food.

Flight
When a woodpecker flies, it flaps its wings a few times, then keeps them closed for a few seconds. This makes the bird rise and fall.

Tail
The woodpecker uses its short tail to brace itself against tree trunks. Each of its tail feathers ends in a stiff point.

Claws
Woodpeckers have short but powerful legs, and feet that work like clamps. They lock themselves into position with their claws before they start to feed.

Green woodpecker
This bird lives in trees, where it is well camouflaged, but it usually flies down to the ground to feed. It has a harsh laughing call that can be heard from a long way away.

Woodpeckers

There are about 200 species of woodpecker, and they live in every continent except Australasia and Antarctica. Instead of perching on branches, woodpeckers cling to tree trunks with their sharp claws. They use their strong beaks to bore holes in trees for nesting. They also use them to communicate with each other by hammering on dead wood.

Acorn woodpecker
In western North America, the acorn woodpecker uses trees as larders. It pecks hundreds of holes in them and stores an acorn in each one as a future food supply.

Toucans

There are 33 species of toucan, found only in South and Central America. The family includes toucans, toucanets, and aracaris. Most have a large beak – up to two-thirds as long as their body. When feeding, a toucan juggles its food in its bill and then tosses its head back before swallowing.

The beak contains lots of air-filled spaces, which make it lighter than it looks.

Red-billed toucan
The Red-billed toucan eats fruit, insects, spiders, and other animals, such as lizards and small birds. It lives in northern South America in the high branches of the rainforest. It usually occurs singly or in pairs.

Tongue curled around skull

Tongue
A woodpecker's tongue can be three or four times as long as its beak, and it has a sticky or spiny tip. The woodpecker flicks it out and uses it to probe for insects. When not in use, the tongue curves right around the back of the skull, just beneath the skin.

Red-billed toucan

Toucan beaks
Toucan beaks are often brightly coloured, this may help birds to identify their own species. The size and colour might also be to frighten away other birds.

Slender tongue

Chestnut-eared aracari
This bird's beak is long and narrow, and gently curved. Both parts have a distinctly serrated edge.

Glossy black beak

Ariel toucan
Found in the southern part of the Amazon rainforest, this toucan feeds on small animals, as well as fruit.

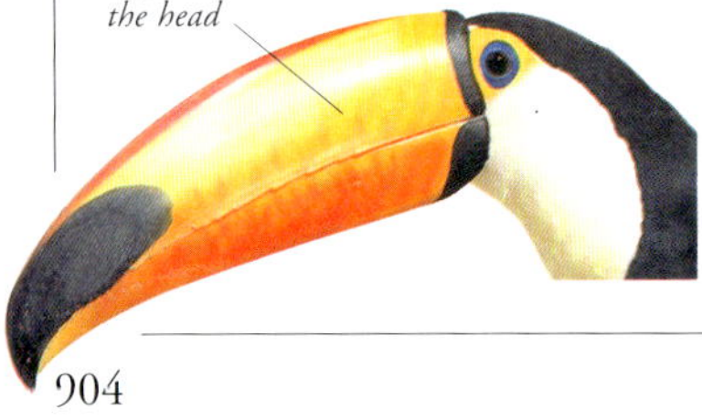

Beak much larger than the head

Toco toucan
This toucan has one of the largest beaks. It can use it to reach fruit on twigs that cannot take its weight.

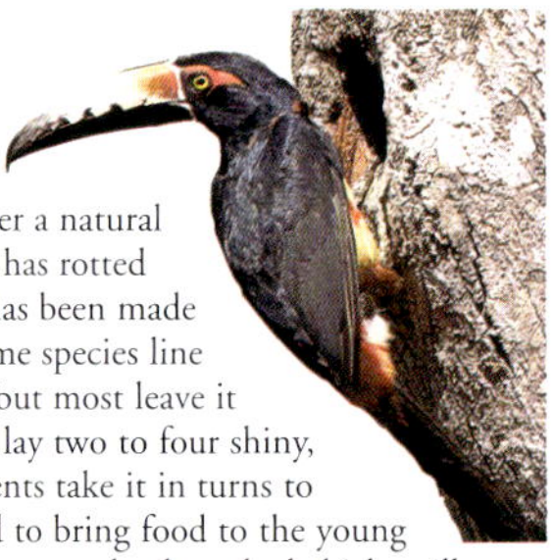

Toucan nests
Toucans nest in tree trunks. They use either a natural hole where the wood has rotted away, or a hole that has been made by a woodpecker. Some species line the hole with leaves, but most leave it bare. Female toucans lay two to four shiny, white eggs. Both parents take it in turns to incubate the eggs and to bring food to the young chicks. After about three weeks the naked chicks will open their eyes, and by about six weeks they will be able to begin to survive on their own.

GREEN WOODPECKER

SCIENTIFIC NAME	*Picus viridis*
ORDER	Piciformes
FAMILY	Picidae
DISTRIBUTION	Europe and western Asia
HABITAT	Woodland and grassy places
DIET	Ants and other insects
SIZE	Length, including tail: 30 cm (12 in)
LIFESPAN	About 7 years

FIND OUT MORE: BIRDS · EGGS · FLIGHT, ANIMAL · KINGFISHERS AND HORNBILLS · NESTS AND BURROWS · WOODLAND WILDLIFE

WORLD WAR I

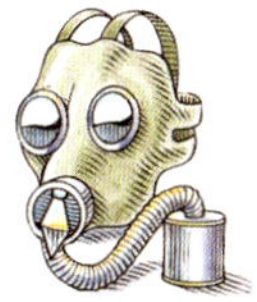

FOR MORE THAN FOUR years, the world was engaged in a war of a ferocity and scale never seen before. The conflict, known then as the Great War and today as World War I, arose out of the economic, colonial, and military rivalry of the European empires. The assassination in 1914 of the heir to one of those empires – Austria-Hungary – was the spark that set the rivalries alight. Within months, fighting had broken out in Europe, Africa, and Asia. By the time the war ended in 1918, the old empires were in ruins, their place taken by a new world power – the USA.

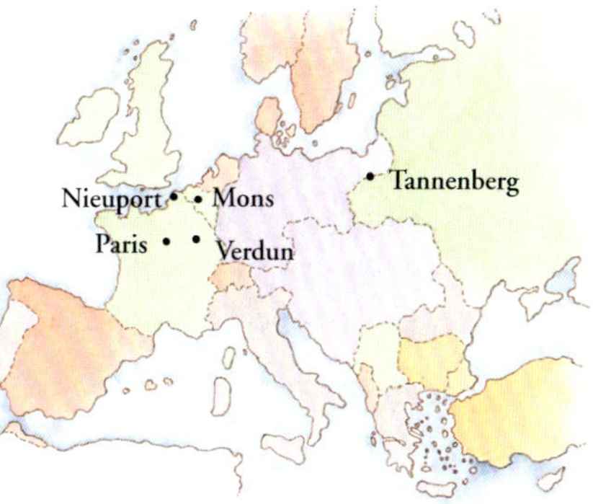

Neutral states
Central powers Austria-Hungary
Central powers Turkish empire
Allies (1914 on)
Allies (1915 on)

Outbreak of war

On 28 June 1914, the heir to the Austrian throne was killed in Serbia. Austria invaded Serbia, Russia came to Serbia's aid, and Germany supported Austria. Fearing war on two fronts, Germany invaded Belgium and France. Britain then declared war on Germany.

Western Front

The German plan was to sweep through Belgium and northern France to capture Paris and knock the French out of the war within weeks. This plan was thwarted by the French army at the River Marne. Both sides then dug lines of defensive trenches, which stretched from the English Channel to the Swiss border, to protect their positions.

Trenches at the Somme

Troops submerged in mud at Passchendaele

The Battle of Passchendaele

The Somme

On 1 July 1916, Allied troops (those on the British and French side) tried to break through German lines near the River Somme, France. By the end of the four-month battle, the Allies had advanced 8 km (5 miles). One million men were killed.

Passchendaele

In July 1917, the Allies tried again to get through German lines, this time near the village of Passchendaele, Belgium. Bad weather turned the area into a sea of mud, over 300,000 Allied troops lost their lives, and hardly any advance was made.

Recruitment

At first, regular troops were reinforced by thousands of volunteers. But as casualty rates soared, governments had to bring in conscription (compulsory military service) to keep up the strength of their armies.

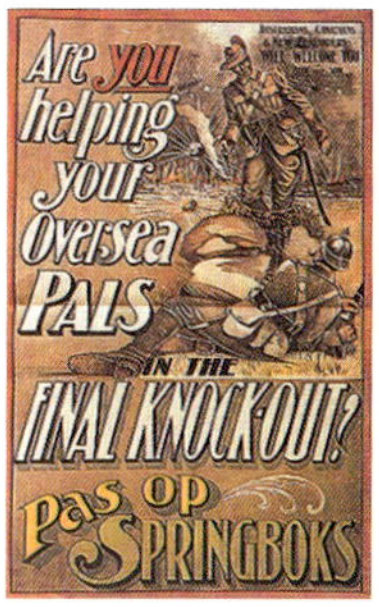

South African recruitment poster

Eastern Fronts

The war in eastern Europe, between Germany and Austria-Hungary on one side, and Russia on the other, was more fluid than in the west. Most battles were held in open country, across what is now Poland and in the eastern Mediterranean. The war expanded into Asia when Turkey attacked Russia at the end of 1914 and the Allies launched the ill-fated Gallipoli campaign. Turkey also posed a threat in Syria and Palestine and so Allied troops were sent from Egypt to defend the region.

British troops in Palestine

Uniform of British Private, Scottish Battalion was khaki-coloured to blend with the mud.

French infantryman's equipment included spare ammunition and food supplies.

Manfred von Richthofen

The most famous pilot of the war was the German airman Manfred von Richthofen (1892–1918). He is said to have destroyed 80 Allied aircraft before he was killed when his aircraft was shot down over France. He was known as the Red Baron because of his bright red Fokker triplane.

Timeline

June 1914 Archduke Franz Ferdinand, heir to the throne of Austria-Hungary, is assassinated; Serbia is blamed.

July 1914 Austria-Hungary invades Serbia in retaliation; France, Germany, and Russia mobilize their armies in preparation for war.

August 1914 Germany declares war on Russia and France and invades Belgium; this brings Britain into the war; Germany pushes back Britain at Mons, Belgium; Germany defeats Russia at Tannenberg.

September 1914 German advance halted by the British and French at the River Marne.

German infantryman

October 1914 Turkey enters the war on the German side; in France a line of defensive trenches is dug, stretching along the Western Front.

April 1915 Germans use poison gas for first time at Ypres, Belgium; Allies try to force Turkey out of war by invading Gallipoli peninsula.

May 1915 Italy joins the war on the Allied side.

The civilian war

The huge armies of World War I needed a massive force of back-up workers to provide them with weapons, food, and other supplies. The entire civilian workforce was directed towards war work, producing arms and ammunition, growing food, and keeping industry and commerce going at home while millions of soldiers fought at the front.

Gas mask

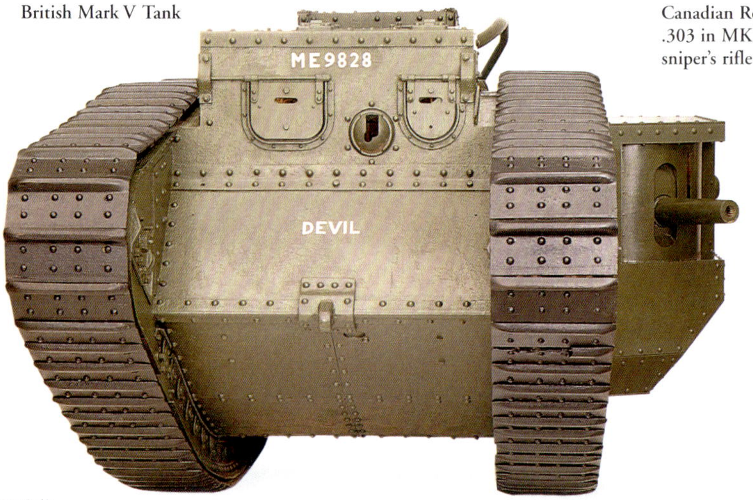

British Mark V Tank

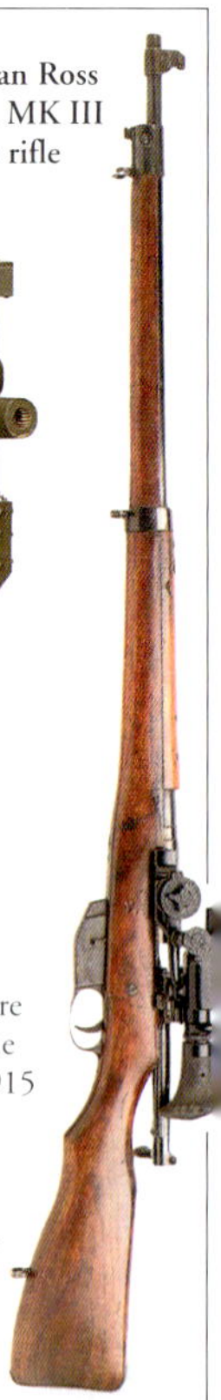

Canadian Ross .303 in MK III sniper's rifle

Women ambulance drivers at the front

World war

World War I was the first truly international war in history. People from every continent took part in the fighting. In Africa and Asia, the Turkish Empire and former German colonies were overrun by British Empire troops. There was also fighting in the Middle East and in the Pacific. The entry of the USA into the war in 1917 marked the end of European dominance of world affairs.

New weapons

The main weapons used in the war were the rifle (with its bayonet), the machine gun, and the artillery shell. In April 1915 the German army introduced a new weapon – gas – which both sides later used to deadly effect. The British first used tanks at the Somme in September 1916, and both sides made more and more use of aircraft – at first for reconnaissance, later for bombing.

Women at war

Before 1914, women traditionally worked in jobs men did not want. During the war, women were required to do jobs normally done by the men fighting at the front. Across Europe, women worked in factories and offices, drove buses and trams, dug fields, and even joined the police forces.

Propaganda

To stiffen morale and weaken the enemy's resistance, both sides used propaganda. People were made to believe the worst of the other side, with leaflets, posters, and radio broadcasts all used for propaganda. Those who refused to fight were given white feathers, a sign of "cowardice".

White feathers

End of the war

In mid-1918, fresh US troops arrived to fight on the Allied side, and there was increasing hunger and discontent among the German soldiers. The Allies broke through the German lines in August 1918. Austria-Hungary and Turkey collapsed in October, and the Allies finally forced Germany to make peace on 11 November 1918.

The Treaty of Versailles

The peace treaty was signed on 28 June 1919 in the palace of Versailles, France. Germany lost territory, and had to limit the size of its army, as well as pay compensation to the Allies. Subsequent treaties redrew the map of eastern Europe.

Signing of the treaty

Poppies

The cost of war

No one knows how many people died in the war. About 9 million soldiers and possibly 13 million civilians were killed. A further 20 million died in the influenza epidemic that swept Europe during 1918–19. Poppies, which grew on the fields of France, became the symbol of those killed in the war.

War art

The horrors of the war inspired painters and poets on both sides. The old romantic idea of war as a great cause was replaced by the realization of its cruelty and destructive force. Many young artists and writers fought at the front; some, such as the British poet Wilfred Owen (1893–1918) were killed in the fighting.

War Landscape by British artist Paul Nash

Timeline

February 1916 German forces try to capture French fortress of Verdun in a 10-month battle.

May 1916 British and German fleets fight inconclusive Battle of Jutland, off Denmark.

French infantryman, 26th Regiment

July–November 1916 Battle of the Somme; tanks used for first time.

April 1917 USA enters war on Allied side.

July–November 1917 Battle of Passchendaele.

March 1918 Germany and Russia make peace at Brest-Litovsk.

March 1918 German forces make massive advances on the Western Front.

July 1918 German advance halted.

August 1918 With the help of American forces, Allied troops make the decisive break through German lines.

Hand-painted camouflage coat

October 1918 Italy defeats Austria-Hungary; both Austria-Hungary and Turkey ask for peace.

November 1918 Armistice signed between Germany and the Allies.

June 1919 Peace treaty signed at Versailles, France. The conditions imposed on Germany were later to become a major cause of World War II.

FIND OUT MORE
Africa, history of
Armies
Empires
Europe, history of
France, history of
Germany, history of
United Kingdom, history of
World War II

WORLD WAR II

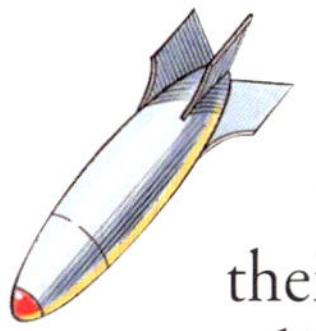

WORLD WAR II WAS the most devastating war in history. For the first time ever in warfare, more civilians than soldiers lost their lives. In total, more than 50 million people were killed, including 20 million Russians, 6 million Poles, and 6 million Jews. The war, which lasted from 1939–45, involved every continent, and few countries or people remained untouched by the carnage. In Europe, the strength of the Russian and American armies was required to defeat Germany. In Asia, atomic warfare was used for the first time to defeat Japan.

How war began

Adolf Hitler took power in Germany in 1933 and set out to restore German power in Europe. He built a strong army and air force, and began to expand German territory in central and eastern Europe. On 1 September, 1939, German troops invaded Poland. In response, Britain and France declared war on Germany.

German Messerschmitt Bf 109E fighter

British Hawker Hurricane Mark 1 fighter

Blitzkrieg

The German army moved tanks quickly into enemy territory, supporting them by aerial bombardment. This strategy, called Blitzkrieg, (lightning war), was successful in 1939–40.

Battle of Britain

For four months in 1940, British aircraft fought against the German air force. After heavy casualties, Germany cancelled its plans to invade Britain.

World war

In June 1941, German troops invaded Russia. Six months later, Japanese aircraft bombed the US naval base at Pearl Harbor, bringing the USA into the war. By the end of 1941, an international alliance of the USA, Russia, and Britain confronted the Axis powers of Germany, Italy, and Japan.

War in Europe

Axis states

Areas controlled by Axis

Allied states

Areas controlled by Allies

Neutral states

Extent of German military occupation

War in the Pacific

Japanese-controlled area by 1942

Extent of Japanese occupation

German tank, 1941

Operation Barbarossa

On 22 June, 1941, 79 German divisions invaded Russia in the biggest military operation in history. At first they made good progress, but Russian resistance ensured that they failed to capture Moscow and Leningrad.

Pearl Harbor

On 7 December, 1941, Japanese planes launched a surprise attack on the American Pacific Fleet stationed at Pearl Harbor in Hawaii, and also invaded the Philippines, Hong Kong, and Malaya. The USA then declared war on both Japan and Germany.

Bombing of the American fleet at Pearl Harbor

Turning point

By mid-1942, the Germans occupied most of Europe and northern Africa, and the Japanese controlled most of the Pacific. Three battles turned the tide: Midway, where the USA stopped the Japanese; El Alamein in North Africa; and Stalingrad, where the Russians began to push back the occupying forces.

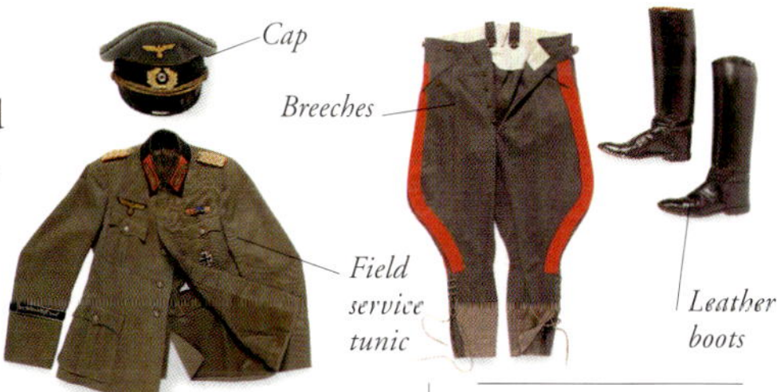

Items from a German officer's uniform

Adolf Hitler

Hitler (1889–1945) became German Chancellor in 1933. He quickly took dictatorial powers and ruled until his death in 1945. His spellbinding oratory convinced many people that he could restore German pride and greatness lost after World War I.

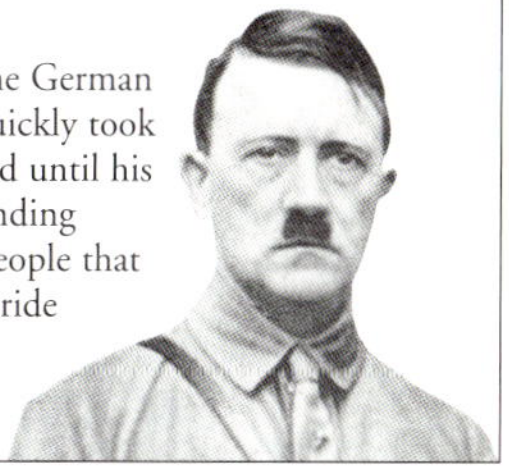

El Alamein

In 1942, German and Italian troops led by Field Marshal Rommel advanced across North Africa towards Egypt and the Suez Canal. In a lengthy battle, the British 8th Army led by General Bernard Montgomery, or "Monty" defeated Rommel at El Alamein, Egypt.

Rommel in North Africa

Timeline

March 1936 Germany begins to expand her territory by sending troops into the Rhineland.

October 1936 Germany and Italy make an alliance – the Rome-Berlin Axis.

November 1936 Germany becomes allied with Japan.

March 1939 German troops invade Czechoslovakia.

Major General, German army

September 1939 Germany and Russia invade Poland; Britain and France declare war on Germany.

April 1940 German troops overrun Denmark and Norway.

May 1940 Germany occupies the Netherlands, Belgium, and France, forcing the British to retreat.

July–October 1940 British air force defeats Germany in the Battle of Britain; preventing Germany's invasion.

Occupied Europe

Life in German-occupied Europe was hard. Food was rationed, newspapers and radio were censored, and everyone was put to work producing supplies for the German war effort. Jews lived in fear of their lives, as more and more of them were rounded up and sent to their deaths in concentration camps, such as Auschwitz and Treblinka.

Resistance

Across Europe, individual people fought to rid their countries of German occupation. In the Netherlands and Denmark, families sheltered Jews in their houses, while in France and Yugoslavia, armed fighters fought a spirited war against the occupying armies.

French resistance fighters

Incendiary bombs

Civilians at war

For the first time, war was brought into the homes of people far away from the battlefield. Bombing of towns and cities meant that civilians became the targets of enemy action and often had to take refuge in shelters. At sea, submarine warfare stopped ships bringing in food and other supplies, causing severe shortages.

Rationing

Shortages all over Europe led to many types of food being rationed. Everyone was given a ration card stating what food they were able to buy each week. People with gardens grew their own food.

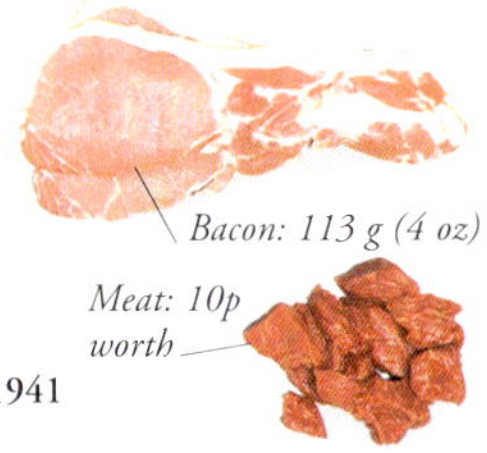

Bacon: 113 g (4 oz)

Meat: 10p worth

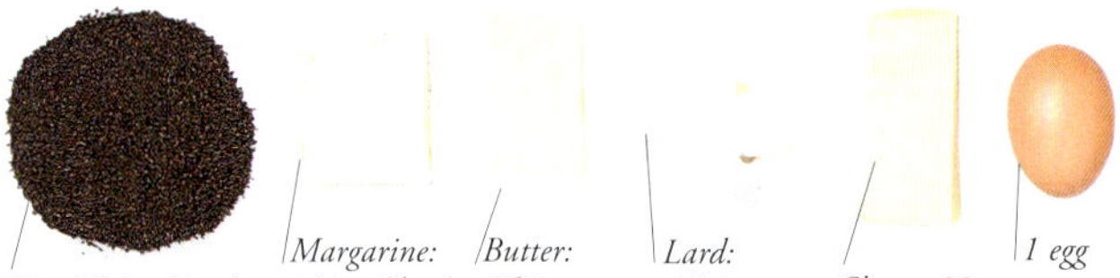

Tea: 56.5 g (2 oz)

Sugar: 226 g (8 oz)

Margarine: 113 g (4 oz)

Butter: 56.5 g (2 oz)

Lard: 56.5 g (2 oz)

Cheese: 28 g (1 oz)

1 egg

Weekly food ration, British adult, 1941

Dresden, after the 1945 air-raid

Air-raids

During 1940–41, the German air force bombed many British cities, and many civilians lost their lives. As the war progressed in favour of the Allies, German cities came under attack. In February 1945, the Allied forces bombed Dresden, and more than 50,000 people were killed.

Winston Churchill

Churchill (1874–1965) became prime minister of Britain in May 1940. A fine orator whose speeches boosted British morale during the Battle of Britain and the rest of the war, Churchill led Britain to victory in 1945, but lost power in July 1945. He was elected prime minister in 1951–55.

Labour camps

In Germany, millions of Jews, gypsies, and prisoners of war were incarcerated in camps. Some camps held slave labourers, who produced munitions and other supplies; others were concentration camps to exterminate Jews and other "undesirables". Conditions were inhumane, and many died of ill-treatment and starvation. Prisoners of war (right) were also often kept in appalling conditions.

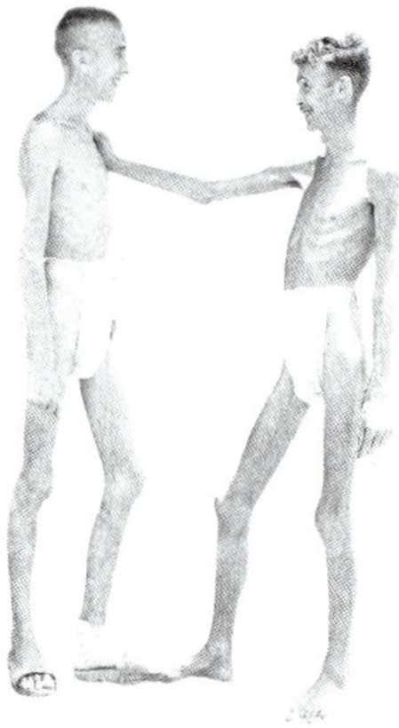

End of the war

By 1944, the war had turned in the Allies' favour. Italy had surrendered, and the Russians were making slow progress towards Berlin. In June 1944, the Allies invaded France, opening up a new western front. The Russians entered Berlin in April 1945, and Germany surrendered in May 1945.

D-Day

On 6 June 1944, more than 100,000 Allied troops, supported by thousands of ships and aircraft, crossed the English Channel and landed on the beaches of France. At first they met fierce German resistance, but by 25 August the Allies had liberated Paris. By the end of the year, they had retaken the whole of France.

Troops landing on D-Day

Railway sign blown off building

Hiroshima

The war against Japan seemed likely to continue as the Japanese fought hard to protect their country. On 6 August, 1945, the US air force dropped an atomic bomb on the Japanese city of Hiroshima, and a second on Nagasaki on 9 August. The Japanese surrendered five days later.

Glass bottle distorted by intense heat

Debris from Hiroshima

December 1941 Japan bombs US Pacific Fleet, leading to US entry into the war.

US serviceman's novel

1942 US fleet stops Japanese advance across the Pacific at the Battle of Coral Sea and the Battle of Midway.

November 1942 British defeat German forces at El Alamein in North Africa.

January 1943 German siege of Stalingrad (Volgograd) broken.

June 1943 Allies invade Italy.

July 1943 Italian fascist dictator Mussolini resigns.

June 1944 D-Day landings: the Allies invade France.

June–August 1944 Russian armies reach Warsaw, Poland, and eastern Prussia.

US serviceman's ration kit

April 1945 Adolf Hitler commits suicide, as the Russian army reaches Berlin.

May 1945 Germany surrenders.

August 1945 Atomic bombs are dropped on the Japanese cities of Hiroshima and Nagasaki; Japan surrenders.

FIND OUT MORE
ARMIES
ASIA, HISTORY OF
EUROPE, HISTORY OF
FRANCE, HISTORY OF
GERMANY, HISTORY OF
HOLOCAUST
UNITED KINGDOM, HISTORY OF
UNITED STATES, HISTORY OF

Worms

WORMS ARE ANIMALS that have an elongated, tube-like body, and no legs. The body of a worm can be cylindrical, flattened, or leaf-like in shape. Worms vary enormously in size and can grow up to 30 metres (100 ft); they include segmented, ribbon, round-worms, and flatworms. We tend to think of these animals as the English naturalist Charles Darwin did – “little ploughmen” worming their way through the soil. However, worms also live in the sea, in fresh water, and as parasites of plants and animals.

Segmented worms

There are three groups of segmented worms. The first group includes the ragworm. The second group includes earthworms and bloodworms (small red freshwater worms living in polluted waters worldwide). The third group includes leeches, which survive by sucking blood from an animal host.

Ragworm

The omnivorous ragworm is a scavenger and a predator, and lives in shallow seashore burrows. Its clearly defined head has tentacles (which grow back if they are cut off), eyes, and a mouth with strong, pincer-like jaws. Bristled paddle-like flaps along each side give it the appearance of a tattered strip of rag. The ragworm moves by swimming or wriggling over surfaces. It is unisexual and usually dies shortly after mating.

King ragworm

Earthworms

The earthworm lives below ground in a burrow. By moving through the soil, eating as it goes, an earthworm allows air and water in, and distributes plant nutrients. When breeding, it produces a cocoon that protects its eggs until they hatch into tiny worms. One cubic metre (35 cubic ft) of grassland may contain 500 worms.

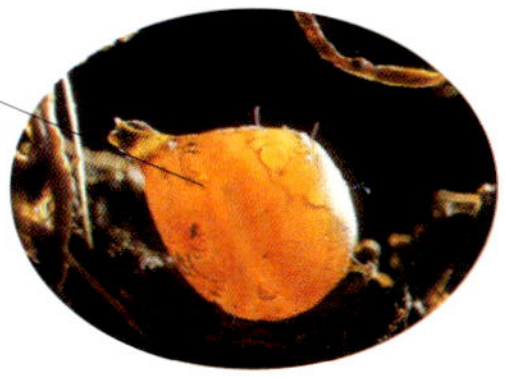

Cocoons, or egg capsules, have up to 20 eggs inside, but usually only one worm develops fully, and emerges.

Peacock worms

These worms live on the shoreline, in tubes made of mud or sand. They have a fan of feathery tentacles around their heads, which withdraw into the tube when they are threatened. One group of peacock worms can create reefs with their sandy tubes.

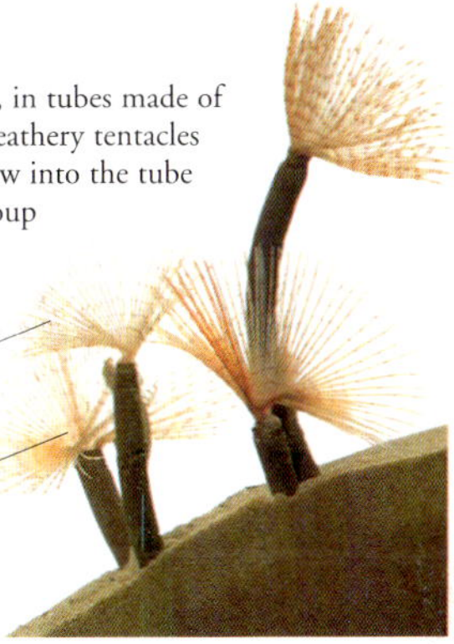

How an earthworm moves

1 The earthworm has a set of circular muscles around its body. It contracts (squeezes) these, which propels the front half of the worm forwards.

2 Muscles running lengthways down the worm's body drag the worm's tail after its head. A mucus covering aids this movement.

Earthworm

Roundworms

Roundworms are unsegmented, spindle-shaped, and usually microscopic. Some roundworms live in the earth – the top 7.5 cms (3 in) of a hectare (2.5 acres) of soil contains up to 7,500 million round-worms. Other round-worms are parasitic, such as the filariasis worm. A single female roundworm can produce up to 200,000 eggs a day.

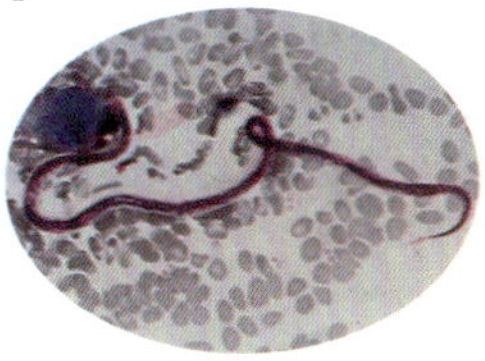

Filariasis worm

Elephantiasis

The roundworm *Wuchereria* causes the filariasis group of diseases. One of these diseases causes grossly enlarged human tissues, and is known as elephantiasis. Elephantiasis occurs when mosquitos infested with the *Wuchereria* larvae bite humans, infecting them with the larvae. The larvae then grow to adult worms within the body. They produce tiny young that they release into the lymph fluid. The larvae block the lymph vessels, and this causes the swelling.

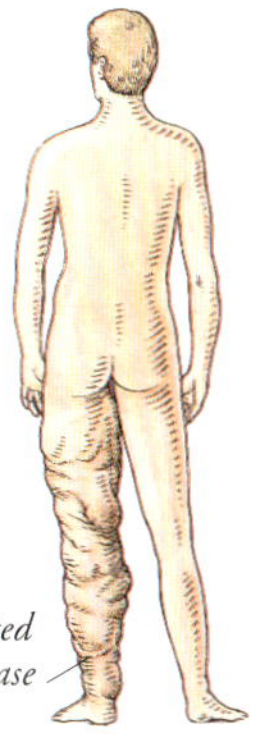

Ribbon worms

Some parasitic forms of worm such as ribbon, bootlace, or horsehair worms lay their eggs in fresh water. When the eggs hatch, the larvae find and infect an insect host. They will then feed on the host until eventually it dies.

Ribbon worm, foraging for food

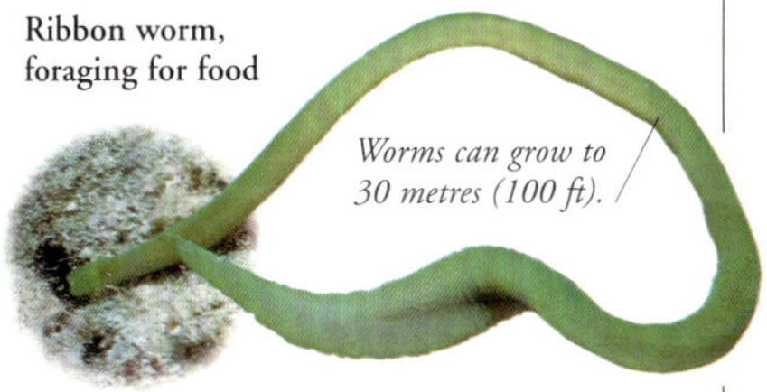

Flatworms

There are three groups of flatworm: planarians, flukes, and tapeworms. The primitive planarians grow into new worms when cut into pieces. The best-known member of the second group is the liver fluke, which infests mammals, snails, and other vertebrates. The third group – tapeworms – includes the human gut tapeworm which can grow to 18 metres (60 ft).

Human gut tapeworm

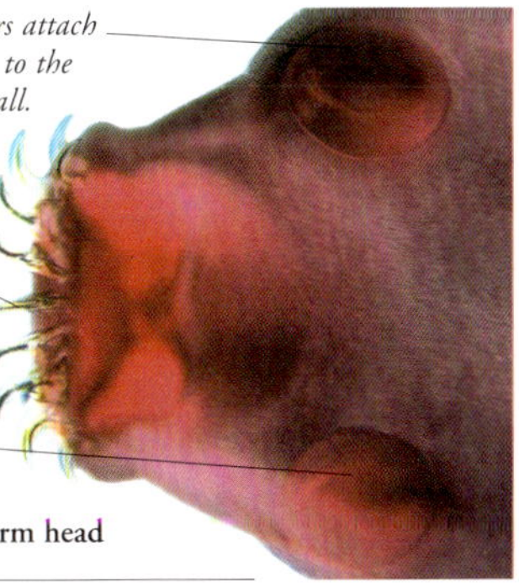

Tapeworm head

King ragworm

- **Scientific name** *Nereis diversicolor*
- **Class** Aclitellata
- **Family** Nereidae
- **Distribution** Seas around western Europe, the Baltic, and Finland
- **Habitat** Sandy, muddy, or rocky shores
- **Diet** Omnivorous, feeding on worms, dead, and dying animals
- **Size** Usually 7–25 cms (10 in), but can grow up to 90 cms (35 in)
- **Lifespan** Up to a year, but often die after spawning

FIND OUT MORE
Coasts
Darwin, Charles
Diseases
Ocean Wildlife
Parasites
Seashore Wildlife

WRITING

COMMUNICATING BY USING MARKS on a surface to represent spoken language is called writing. Its vital importance lies in its power to preserve thoughts and ideas that would otherwise be lost. Thousands of scripts have been invented, each expressing a different language or adapted to a particular surface, be it clay, wood, stone, or paper. Writing not only conveys meaning – it can also be beautiful in itself. The art of fine script is called calligraphy.

Writing implements

Throughout history, writers have used many different kinds of tools, each one suited to the most commonly available writing surface. The kind of mark each tool makes profoundly affects the nature of the script.

Stick and clay

The first writing was devised by the Sumerians 5,000 years ago. They used sticks called styluses to make triangular marks in soft clay, which was then baked hard.

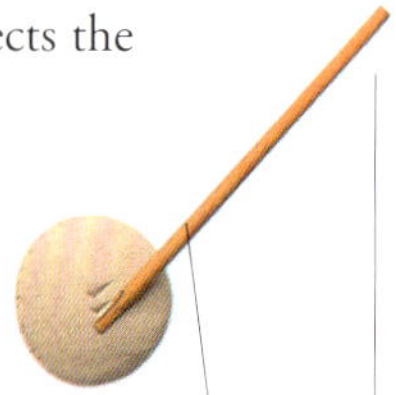

Stylus

Pen and ink

For centuries, people wrote on paper, using pens repeatedly dipped in ink. Early pens were trimmed goose quills. Later pens had metal nibs.

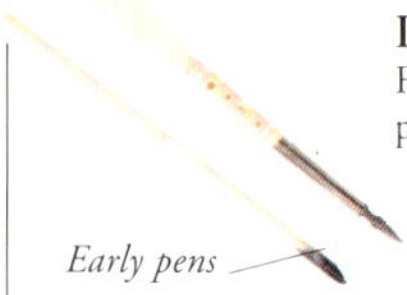

Early pens

Ballpoint pens

A ballpoint is a disposable pen that has a small ballbearing as a writing point, and an internal ink supply. One of the world's most-used ballpoint pens is the biro, patented in 1943.

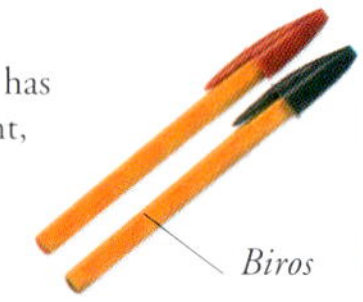

Biros

Monumental inscription in Latin

Roman alphabet

The ancient Romans evolved a new alphabet to write Latin. The alphabet had 21 characters, and each represented a different sound. It was written in either upper case (capital) or lower case (small) letters. Today, the influence of the Roman Empire can be seen throughout Europe. Most of the languages of western Europe, such as English, are written in the Roman alphabet, now with 26 characters.

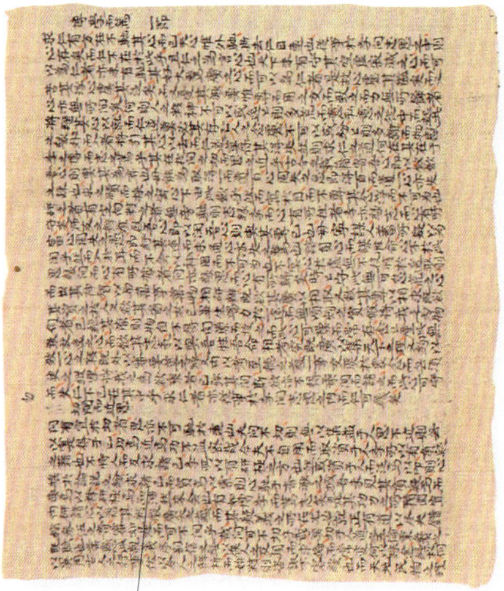

Chinese passage skillfully written on silk

Scripts

All writing consists of a series of marks, or characters, which make up a script. In some scripts, such as Chinese, each character carries the meaning of a spoken word. In alphabetic scripts, such as Latin or English, each character represents a sound, and must be fitted with others to make a word.

Chinese

Chinese has the longest history of all current writing systems, stretching back to at least 1500 BC. Each character represents a different word, so many thousands must be learned before even simple passages can be read. Traditional Chinese is written with brush and ink on paper.

The fluent lines of Arabic give beauty to each word.

Arabic

Arabic has 17 basic characters, written from right to left. Dots are added to create the 28 letters of the Arabic alphabet. The letters are joined with curved strokes, and there are further bold strokes at the end of each word. This gives Arabic an urgent sense of movement from right to left. The Qur'an, the holy book of Islam, teaches that writing is a gift from God. As well as using writing practically, to provide information, it is also used as decoration (like Chinese, Arabic calligraphy is a prized art form). Texts from the Qur'an are inscribed on mosque walls.

Unknown scripts

There are many ancient scripts that are no longer understood. Language experts work for years trying to decipher them. No one could read Egyptian hieroglyphics until the Frenchman Jean-François Champollion (1790–1832) deciphered them in 1824.

Mayan glyphs carved in stone

Rounded, stylized symbols

Mayan glyphs

Between AD 300 and 1500, the Mayans of Central America produced thousands of carved stone inscriptions. Many of the 850 characters, or glyphs, clearly represent animals and objects, but others are abstract symbols. Very little Mayan writing was deciphered until the 1960s, when the life histories of Mayan rulers were first translated. About 85 per cent of gylphs can now be understood.

Shorthand

Words are spoken much faster than they can be written, and for people such as reporters it is useful to learn a quick way of jotting them down quickly and accurately. Shorthand systems replace words and phrases with brief marks, that can be read and understood later. Today, shorthand has largely been superceded by tape recorders and dictaphones.

Timeline

3100 BC Sumerians develop first writing system using pictograms (picture symbols of people, animals, and objects).

Pictograms

3000 BC Egyptians develop hieroglyphics.

1800 BC Chinese characters, similar to those in use today, are written on tortoise shells.

c. 1000 BC Greeks invent the first alphabetic script, where each character (letter) represents a sound, and letters combine to form words.

c.63 BC A Latin form of shorthand (a kind of speedwriting) is invented: it is used for 1,000 years.

1905 After 5,000 years, linguists produce the first modern translation of the Sumerian writing system.

FIND OUT MORE

EGYPT, ANCIENT
LANGUAGES
MAYA
ROMAN EMPIRE
SIGNS AND SYMBOLS

X-RAYS AND THE ELECTROMAGNETIC SPECTRUM

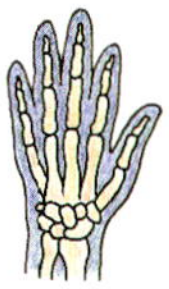

INVISIBLE WAVES OF ENERGY called X-rays allow doctors to see through the soft tissues of the human body, enabling them to diagnose disease and injury without resorting to surgery. X-rays are a type of wave energy called electromagnetic radiation. They form just one part of a whole range of electromagnetic radiation called the electromagnetic spectrum, which also includes radio waves and light.

Electromagnetic radiation

The true nature of electromagnetic radiation still puzzles scientists, because it travels as waves of energy but also seems to be made up of tiny energy particles. This energy can travel through many types of matter, and also through a vacuum.

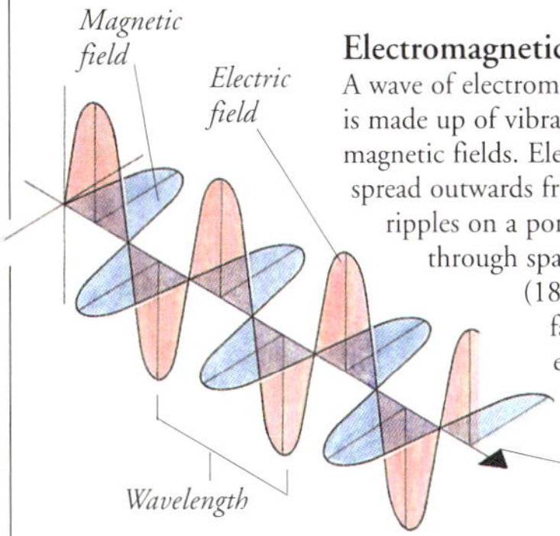

Electromagnetic waves

A wave of electromagnetic radiation is made up of vibrating electric and magnetic fields. Electromagnetic waves spread outwards from a source, like ripples on a pond. They travel through space at 299,792.5 km/s (186,287.5 miles/s) – faster than anything else in the Universe.

Photons

Scientists think that the energy carried by electromagnetic waves is split up into particle-like units called photons. They are often described as "wave packets". An electromagnetic wave probably consists of a stream of photons.

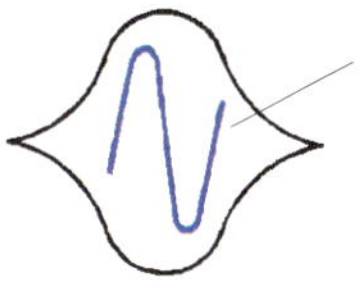

Photon of red light

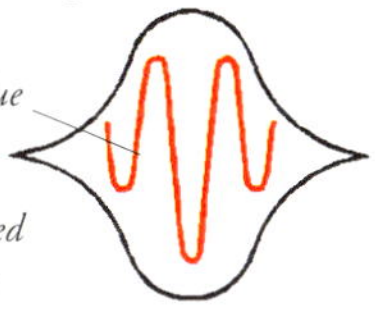

Photon of blue light

James Clerk Maxwell

The Scottish physicist James Clerk Maxwell (1831–79) was the first to realize that light is a form of electromagnetic radiation. In 1864, he used mathematical equations to prove the existence of the electromagnetic spectrum. Maxwell also studied colour and colour blindness.

Solar radiation

The Sun gives out a wide range of electromagnetic radiation that travels through space and reaches the Earth. Most of this radiation is absorbed by gases in the Earth's atmosphere, but radio waves, the visible spectrum, and some infrared and ultraviolet are able to pass through.

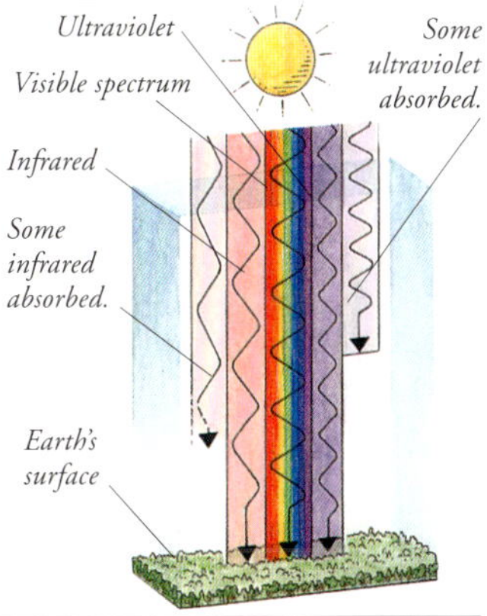

Timeline

1667 English scientist Isaac Newton splits white light into the visible spectrum.

1800 William Herschel, a German-born astronomer, discovers infrared rays.

1801 German physicist Johann Ritter discovers ultraviolet radiation.

1864 Maxwell proves that the electromagnetic spectrum exists, and that electromagnetic radiation is caused by the link between electricity and magnetism.

1887 German physicist Heinrich Hertz makes radio waves artificially.

1895 German physicist Wilhelm Röntgen discovers X-rays.

1896 First medical X-ray taken by American scientist Michael Pupin.

1900 French physicist Paul Villard is the first to detect gamma rays.

1901 Italian inventor Guglielmo Marconi sends the first radio signal across the Atlantic.

1947 Microwave ovens on sale in the USA.

Electromagnetic spectrum

Each type of electromagnetic radiation has a different wavelength and frequency (number of waves per second). Waves with the shortest wavelengths and the highest frequencies have the most energy.

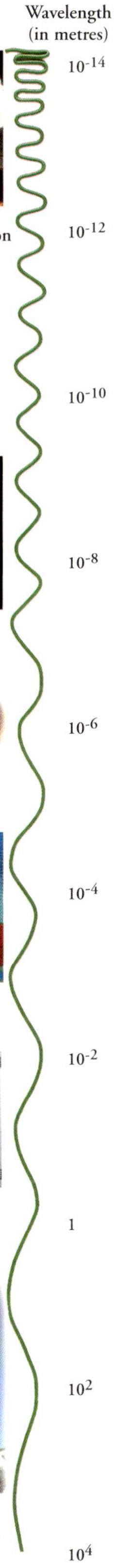

Gamma rays

The nuclei (centres) of radioactive atoms give out gamma rays during nuclear reactions and explosions. These high-energy rays are very penetrating and can damage human cells as they pass through the body.

Nuclear bomb explosion

X-rays

An X-ray photograph shows the denser parts of the human body as light areas on a dark background. X-rays can pass through flesh, but are blocked by teeth, bones, and some organs.

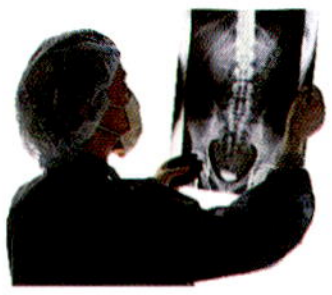

X-ray photograph

Ultraviolet

A substance that absorbs the energy of ultraviolet waves and immediately releases it again as visible light is said to be fluorescent. A fluorescent rock glows in the dark when exposed to ultraviolet waves.

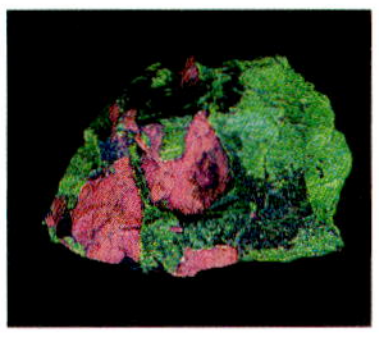

Fluorescent rock

Visible spectrum

Light is the only type of electromagnetic radiation visible to human eyes. Light includes all the colours of the rainbow, which together are called the visible spectrum.

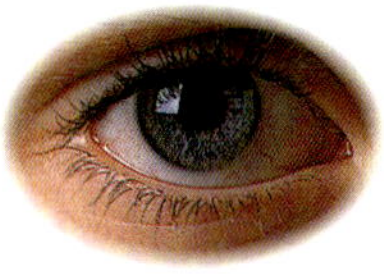

Human eye

Infrared

All warm objects give out infrared rays. Photographs called thermographs record these rays and show the warm and cool parts of an object as different colours, from yellow (hottest) to blue (coldest).

Infrared photograph

Microwaves

Microwaves are actually short-wavelength radio waves. A microwave oven uses microwaves to cook food that contains water. The water molecules absorb the energy of the microwaves and vibrate faster, heating up the food.

Microwave oven

Radio waves

Electromagnetic waves with the lowest energy are called radio waves. They can have wavelengths of thousands of kilometres. These waves are easy to produce using an electrical device called an oscillator. Radio waves are used to transmit radio and television programmes.

Radio masts

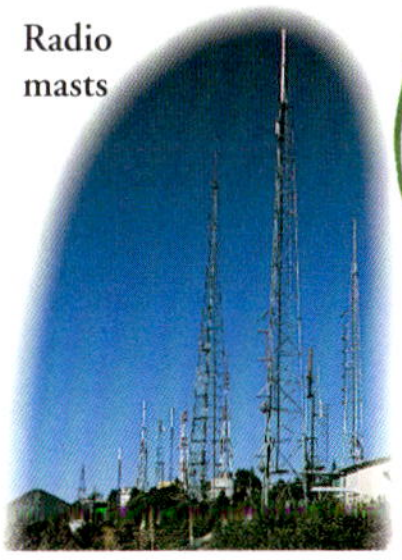

FIND OUT MORE: COLOUR · ELECTRICITY · ELECTROMAGNETISM · ENERGY · HEAT AND TEMPERATURE · LIGHT · MAGNETISM · RADIOACTIVITY

ZOOS

HUMANS HAVE ALWAYS been fascinated by animals, and their lifestyles. Since ancient times, animals have been kept in captivity. Today, many cities have a zoo, or zoological garden, where animals are kept for exhibition. In recent years, zoos have been criticized by those who believe it is wrong to keep animals in captivity. However, others argue that zoos can play a part in conservation.

Zoo history

Humans have kept animals for at least 25,000 years. Possibly the first animals kept purely out of curiosity were pigeons in Iraq over 6,500 years ago. The first animal collection was probably that of the ancient Egyptians over 4,000 years ago. It contained 100 elephants, 70 big cats, and thousands of other mammals. Rulers in China also established a huge zoo, called the Gardens of Intelligence, about 3,000 years ago. In the past, animals were often taught to perform for visitors; this rarely happens today.

London Zoo
In 1828, a small corner of Regent's Park was set aside for the use of the Zoological Society of London. The society's aim was to "interest and amuse the public". However, the zoo soon took on more serious scientific work concerned with living animals.

The role of a zoo

Zoos have three main aims: education, conservation, and research. Least important, is entertainment for the public. In this way, zoos help to protect animals instead of exploiting them. Organizations such as Zoo Check, in the UK, make sure the animals are given proper care, monitoring the animals' diet, enclosures, and physical and mental health.

Children watching rabbits from "rabbit hole".

Education
As our access to the wild decreases, so does our contact with animals. For many people zoos are the only place where they can experience contact with animals. Zoos educate children to appreciate animals and the threats they face.

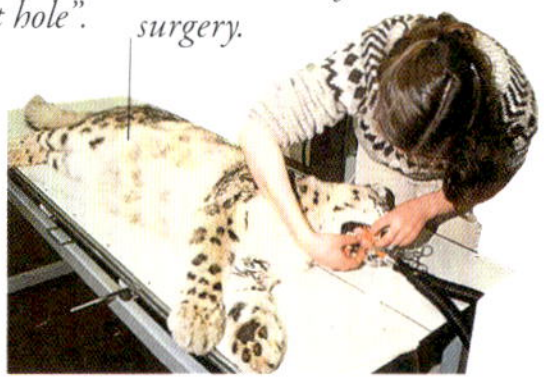

Snow leopard under anaesthetic before surgery.

Animal welfare
The health of zoo animals is very important. Animals are encouraged to behave as they would in the wild. For example, chimps are given logs containing crickets for them to extract. Without this stimulation, animals get bored and start behaving abnormally.

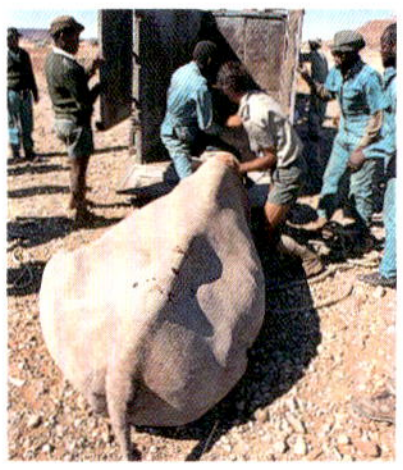

Conservation
Due to habitat destruction, the only chance for many animals of avoiding extinction is to be kept and bred in captivity. Many species from rhinos to crickets have been bred in zoos and successfully returned to the wild.

Penguin wearing tracking device to monitor its movements in Antarctica.

Research
Zoos carry out research involved in developing pregnancy test kits for rhinos, treating illnesses, artificially inseminating animals, and tracking animals in the wild.

Greenhouse for growing food for locusts and other invertebrates.

These rainforest trees are normally found in the animal's natural habitat.

Glass sides for all round visibility

Breeding units for endangered species

Twilight world – dark cave setting for nocturnal invertebrates

Layered walkways allow animals to be observed at all levels of the trees.

Model of proposed new invertebrate house for London Zoo

Zoo of the future

With changing attitudes to animals kept in captivity and advances in technology, zoos are becoming more sophisticated. New enclosures are planned that simulate conditions in the animals' natural habitat. This is done both for the animals' welfare and so visitors can see animals in conditions similar to those in the wild. The combination of species, type of vegetation, temperature, and humidity are all considered. Food is hidden to encourage animals to forage, as they would in the wild.

Wildlife parks

Many people disagree with keeping animals behind bars. Most city zoos do not have enough space to keep animals in more natural settings; as a result, wildlife parks were developed. One of the first was Whipsnade Park Zoo, in the UK. With over 230 ha (567 acres), large animals can roam around in herds in more natural settings. Animals from the same country are often put together, making them feel more at home and giving the visitor a better idea of what they look like in the wild.

Giraffes in safari park

Sea-life centres
Aquatic animals need very specialist care so specially designed sea-life centres, or aquariums, have been built. In many of these centres the public get the opportunity to touch certain marine animals, something that is almost impossible in the wild. Sea-life centres primarily concentrate on displaying marine animals local to the area in which they are situated. However, some also have more exotic animals. Many people are unhappy about keeping large marine animals, such as dolphins and the orca, in captivity.

Killer whale in aquarium

FIND OUT MORE
ANIMAL BEHAVIOUR · ANIMALS · CONSERVATION · ELEPHANTS · GIRAFFES · PENGUINS · RHINOCEROSES AND TAPIRS · WHALES AND DOLPHINS

REFERENCE SECTION

CLASSIFYING LIVING THINGS

BIOLOGISTS CLASSIFY LIVING things into large groups, called kingdoms. Each kingdom is then subdivided into several smaller groups. The classification chart on these pages shows the five kingdoms, together with most of the smaller groups that make up the living world.

KEY

Each kingdom is divided into several smaller groups: phyla, sub-phyla, classes, orders, and divisions. A division is the plant equivalent of a phylum. The chart is colour-coded to show how the groups relate to each other.

- Kingdom
- Phylum
- Sub-phylum
- Class
- Order
- Division

Scientific names

Every species has a two-part scientific name that is the same worldwide. The first part of the name gives the genus; the second part the species. All numbers of species are approximate, as many more species still await discovery.

Classifying a species

Living things are classified according to the features they have in common. Kingdoms are the largest groups in the classification system, and species are the smallest groups. Each species contains a group of living things that can breed together. The chart below shows how biologists would classify one species – the tiger – in the animal kingdom.

Kingdom Animals (Animalia)
A kingdom is the largest grouping in the classification of living things.

Phylum Chordates (Chordata)
A phylum is a major group within a kingdom. It is sometimes called a division in the classification of plants.

Class Mammals (Mammalia)
A class is a major part of a phylum or sub-phylum. A sub-class is a large group within a class.

Order Carnivores (Carnivora)
An order is part of a class or sub-class.

Family Cats (Felidae)
A family is a large collection of species that have several features in common.

Genus Big cats (*Panthera*)
A genus is a small collection of similar species.

Species Tiger
(*Panthera tigris*)

Protists

This kingdom contains simple organisms that mostly have a single cell. There are at least 65,000 species.

PROTISTS
(PROTISTA)

Ciliate

- AMOEBAS (Sarcodina) 20,000 species
- FLAGELLATES (Zoomastigina) 15,000 species
- CILIATES (Ciliophora) 8,000 species
- SPOROZOANS (Sporozoa) 5,000 species
- ALGAE (Several phyla) 20,000 species

MONERANS
(MONERA)

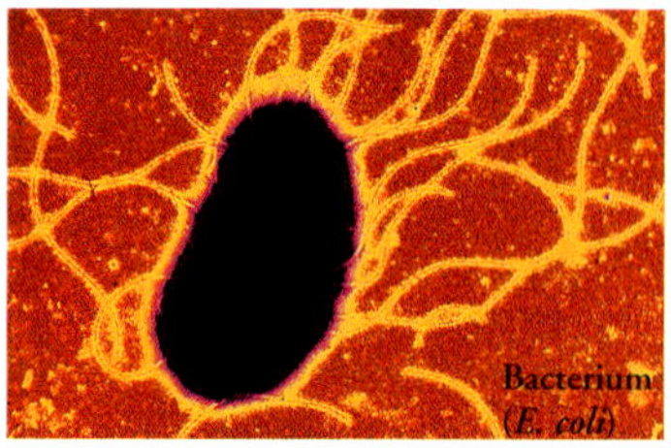

Bacterium (*E. coli*)

Monerans

This kingdom includes the single-celled organisms, such as bacteria. Monerans were the first life forms, and there are now over 5,000 species. It also covers blue-green algae.

- PRIMITIVE BACTERIA (Archaebacteria) 500 species
- TYPICAL BACTERIA (Eubacteria) 5,000 species

Plants

Plants cannot move; they reproduce by making spores or seeds. The kingdom contains more than 400,000 species.

PLANTS
(PLANTAE)

Cushion moss

Fern

FLOWERING PLANTS (Angiospermophyta)

Yellow yarrow

Delphiniums

- MONOCOTYLEDONS 80,000 species
- DICOTYLEDONS 170,000 species
- MOSSES AND LIVERWORTS (Bryophyta) 15,000 species
- CLUB MOSSES (Lycopodophyta) 1,000 species
- HORSETAILS (Sphenophyta) 15 species
- FERNS (Pteridophyta) 12,000 species
- GYMNOSPERMS (Gymnospermophyta) about 1,000 species
- CONIFERS (Coniferopsida) 500 species
- CYCADS (Cycadopsida) 100 species
- JOINT PINES (Gnetopsida) 70 species

FUNGI
(FUNGI)

Saffron milk caps

Fungi

Fungi absorb food made by plants and animals. There are many thousands of species, classified into several phyla.

- FUNGI IMPERFECTI (Deuteromycota) 25,000 species
- CLUB FUNGI (Basidiomycota) 25,000 species
- SAC FUNGI (Ascomycota) 30,000 species
- MOULDS (Zygomycota) 750 species
- WATER MOULDS (Oomycota) 600 species

ANIMALS (ANIMALIA)

Animals
The animal kingdom contains organisms that cannot make their own food. Most animals can move around, but some spend their adult lives in one place.

ROTIFERS (Rotifera) 2,000 species

MOSS ANIMALS (Bryozoa) 4,000 species

c.13 OTHER SMALL PHYLA c.2,000 species

VELVETWORMS (Onychophora) 100 species

SPONGES (Porifera) 9,000 species

COMB JELLIES (Ctenophora) 90 species

WORMS, LEECHES (Annelida) 18,600 species

MOLLUSCS (Mollusca) 110,000 species

- OCTOPUSES, SQUIDS (Cephalopoda) 600 species
- SOLENOGASTERS (Aplacophora) 250 species
- MUSSELS, CLAMS (Bivalvia) 15,000 species
- SNAILS (Gastropoda) 35,000 species
- DEEP-SEA LIMPETS (Monoplacophora) 10 species
- TUSK SHELLS (Scaphopoda) 350 species
- CHITONS (Polyplacophora) 500 species

Octopus

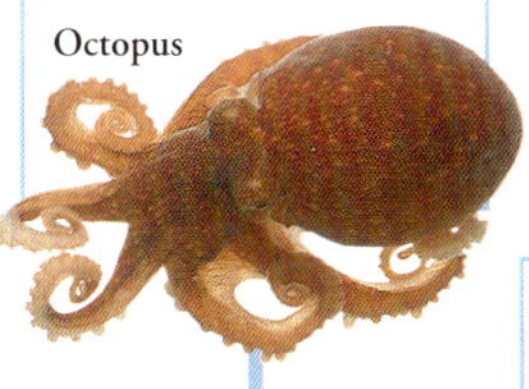

ECHINODERMS (Echinodermata) 6,000 species

- SEA URCHINS (Echinoidea) 950 species
- STARFISH (Asteroidea) 1,500 species
- BRITTLE STARS (Ophiuroidea) 2,000 species
- SEA CUCUMBERS (Holothuroidea) 900 species

ROUNDWORMS (Nematoda) 20,000 species

HORSEHAIR WORMS (Nematomorpha) 250 species

WATERBEARS (Tardigrada) 600 species

LAMPSHELLS (Brachiopoda) 300 species

FLATWORMS, FLUKES, TAPEWORMS (Platyhelminthes) 15,000 species

SEA ANEMONES, HYDRAS, CORALS, JELLYFISH (Cnidaria) 9,500 species

SPINY-HEADED WORMS (Acanthocephala) 1,500 species

ARTHROPODS (Arthropoda) at least 1,000,000 species

- SEA SPIDERS (Pycnogonida) 1,000 species
- CENTIPEDES (Chilopoda) 2,500 species
- MILLIPEDES (Diplopoda) 10,000 species
- HORSESHOE CRABS (Merostomata) 4 species

ARACHNIDS (Arachnida) 73,000 species

Camel spiders
Harvestmen
Micro-whip scorpions
Mites and ticks
Pseudoscorpions

Scorpion

Scorpions
Spiders
Tail-less whip scorpions
Tick spiders
Whip scorpions

INSECTS (Insecta) at least 1,000,000 species

Ants, bees, wasps
Beetles
Booklice
Bristletails
Bugs
Butterflies and moths
Caddis flies
Cockroaches
Diplurans
Dragonflies
Earwigs
Fleas
Flies
Grasshoppers, crickets
Grylloblattids
Lacewings and antlions
Lice
Mayflies
Praying mantids
Scorpion flies
Silverfish
Springtails
Stick and leaf insects
Stoneflies
Stylopids
Termites
Thrips
Webspinners
Zorapterans

Morpho butterfly

CRUSTACEANS (Crustacea) 40,000 species

- BRANCHIOPODS (Branchiopoda) 1,000 species
- BARNACLES (Cirripedia) 1,220 species
- SPINY SAND SHRIMPS (Branchiura) 125 species
- SAND SHRIMPS (Cephalocarida) 9 species
- MYSTACOCARIDEANS (Mystacocarida) 10 species
- CRABS, LOBSTERS, AND SHRIMPS (Malacostraca) 20,000 species

Crab

- MUSSEL SHRIMPS (Ostracoda) 2,000 species
- COPEPODS (Copepoda) 7,500 species

CHORDATES (Chordata) 45,000 species

AMPHIBIANS (Amphibia) 4,200 species

Caecilians
Frogs and toads
Newts and salamanders

REPTILES (Reptilia) 6,000 species

Crocodilians
Lizards and snakes
Tuatara
Turtles, tortoises, and terrapins

Red-tailed racer

BONY FISH (Osteichthyes) 20,000 species

More than 20 orders including:
Carp
Catfish
Eels
Flying fish
Herrings, anchovies
Perch, marlins, swordfish, tunas
Salmon, trout

Clown fish

JAWLESS FISH (Agnatha) 75 species

SEA SQUIRTS (Ascidiacea) 2,500 species

SHARKS AND RAYS (Chondrichthyes) 800 species

Sharks, dolphins
Skates, rays

MAMMALS (Mammalia) 4,600 species

Aardvarks
Bats
Carnivores
Edentates (anteaters, armadillos, sloths)
Elephants
Elephant shrews
Even-toed hoofed mammals
Flying lemurs
Hares, rabbits, pikas
Hyraxes
Insectivores
Marsupials (pouched mammals)
Monotremes (egg-laying mammals)
Odd-toed hoofed mammals
Pangolins
Primates
Rodents
Seals, sea lions, walruses
Sea cows
Tree shrews
Whales and dolphins

Silverback gorilla

BIRDS (Aves) 9,000 species

Albatrosses, petrels, shearwaters, fulmars
Cassowaries, emus
Cranes, rails, coots, bustards
Cuckoos, roadrunners
Divers or loons
Ducks, geese, swans
Eagles, hawks, vultures, falcons, kites, buzzards
Grebes
Herons, storks, ibises, flamingos
Kingfishers, bee-eaters, rollers
Kiwis
Mousebirds
Nightjars, frogmouths
Ostriches
Owls
Parrots
Passerines
Pelicans, gannets, cormorants, frigate birds, darters
Penguins
Pheasants, partridges, grouse, turkeys
Pigeons, doves
Rheas
Sandgrouse
Swifts, hummingbirds
Tinamous
Trogons
Turacos
Wading birds, gulls, terns, auks
Woodpeckers, toucans, barbets, honeyguides, puffbirds, jacamars

Orange weaver

HOW LIVING THINGS WORK

ALL LIVING THINGS have characteristics in common: they grow, feed, reproduce, use energy, and respond to the outside world. Most living things have developed senses and patterns of behaviour that ensure the survival of their species.

REPRODUCTION RATES

Some animals can reproduce extremely rapidly, but only a few of their offspring survive to become adults.

SPECIES	BREEDING AGE	OFFSPRING PER YEAR
Fruit fly	10–14 days	Up to 900
Mouse	6 weeks	50–70
Rabbit	8 months	10–30
Northern gannet	5–6 years	1
Nile crocodile	15 years	50

Fourteen-day-old mice

ANIMAL SPEEDS

AIR	Dragonfly 58 kmh (36 mph) Fastest-flying insect	Frigate bird 153 kmh (95 mph)	Spine-tailed swift 170 kmh (106 mph) Fastest-flying bird	Peregrine falcon 200 kmh (124 mph) Fastest bird in a dive
LAND	American cockroach 5 kmh (3 mph) Fastest-running insect	Ostrich 72 kmh (45 mph) Fastest-running bird	Pronghorn antelope 86 kmh (53 mph) Fastest mammal over long distances	Cheetah 96.5 kmh (60 mph) Fastest mammal over short distances
SEA	Gentoo penguin 35 kmh (22 mph) Fastest-swimming bird	Killer whale 55 kmh (34.5 mph) Fastest-swimming mammal	Marlin 80 kmh (50 mph)	Sailfish 109 kmh (68 mph)

Dragonfly

Male ostrich

Peregrine falcon

Cheetah

Gentoo penguin

Black marlin

PLANT AND ANIMAL LIFESPANS

The chart below shows how long different animals and plants live. The ages given are the maximum average lifespans.

BACTERIA	20 mins
PROTISTS	Several days
FUNGI	Fairy ring mushroom (5 days); Hyphae of honey fungus (10 years)
CONIFERS	Cedar of Lebanon (500 years); Yew (3,500 years)
FLOWERING PLANTS	Foxglove (2 years); Bamboo (30–60 years); Saguaro cactus (150 years); English oak (1,500 years)
ARTHROPODS	Housefly (17–30 days); Queen ant (15 years)
FISH	Goldfish (10–25 years); Lake sturgeon (50–80 years)
AMPHIBIANS	Smooth newt (15 years); Fire salamander (20 years); Common toad (40 years)
REPTILES	Boa constrictor (40 years); American alligator (60 years); Tuatara (101 years); Giant tortoise (150 years)
BIRDS	Starling (1 year); Wandering albatross (60 years); Andean condor (70 years)
MAMMALS	Red fox (8 years); Giraffe (20 years); African elephant (70 years); Killer whale (90 years)

Bacteria

Honey fungus

Bamboo

Yew tree

Foxglove

Housefly

English oak

Toad

Fire salamander

Giant tortoise

Red fox

African elephant

Andean condor

LIFESPAN FACTS

- The shrew has the shortest lifespan of all mammals. Shrews normally live for only 12–18 months in the wild.
- Humans are the longest-living mammals. The oldest elephant on record lived to the age of 82 in Sri Lanka.

Shrew

- Giant tortoises are the longest-living reptiles. The oldest tortoise ever recorded came from the Seychelles. It lived to the age of 152.
- The giant marine clam (Tridacna) is the longest-living animal in the world. It can live to be more than 200 years old.

Giant clam

Body temperatures

The chart below shows the average body temperatures of exothermic ("cold-blooded") and endothermic ("warm-blooded") animals.

Exothermic ("cold-blooded") animals

-2°C (28.4°F) | 0°C (32°F) | 5°C (41°F) | 10°C (50°F) | 15°C (59°F) | 20°C (68°F) | 25°C (77°F) | 30°C (86°F) | 35°C (95°F) | 40°C (104°F) | 45°C (130°F)

Ice-fish

Ice-fish -2°C–2°C (28.4°F–35.6°F)

Salmon 0°C–20°C (32°F–68°F)

Frog 7°C–30°C (44°F–86°F)

Desert pupfish 34°C (93.2°F)

Lizard 18°C–45°C (64.4°F–113°F)

Temperature facts

- A hibernating animal's blood temperature can drop to 0°C.
- Cold-blooded animals, such as spiders, may live for weeks without food.

Endothermic ("warm-blooded") animals

Bat 28°C (82.4°F)

Spiny anteater 30°C (86°F)

Hedgehog 35°C (95°F)

Human 37°C (98.6°F)

Bird 40°C (104°F)

Gestation periods

The gestation period is the amount of time young take to develop inside the mother. Large mammals usually have long gestation periods, although kangaroos have gestation periods of only 33 days.

Longest gestation periods

Mammal	Average gestation (days)
African elephant	660
Asian elephant	660
Baird's beaked whale	520
White rhinoceros	490
Walrus	480
Giraffe	460
Tapir	400

Giraffes

Shortest gestation periods

Mammal	Average gestation (days)
Short-nosed bandicoot	12
Opossum	13
Shrew	14
Golden hamster	15
Lemming	16
Mouse	20

Opossum

Gestation fact

- The 480-day gestation of the walrus includes a delay of up to five months so that the young can be delivered at the most favourable time of the year.

Walruses

Animal energy needs

The chart below shows how many kilojoules (kJ) different animal species need per day for a moderate amount of activity.

Animal	kJ required
House mouse	45.4
European robin	89.9
Grey squirrel	386
Domestic cat	1,554
Female human	10,080
Male human	13,713
Llama	16,128
Tiger	33,600
Giraffe	152,754
Walrus	159,852
Asian elephant	256,872

Energy fact

- A flea can jump more than 100 times its own height using energy stored in pads in its leg joints.

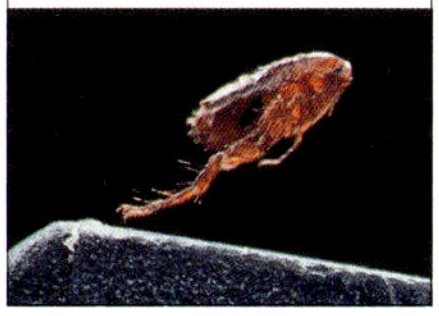

Flea jumping

Animal heart rates

Animals with small bodies have much faster heartbeats than animals with larger bodies.

Animal	Beats per minute
Grey whale	9
Harbour seal (diving)	10
Elephant	25
Human	70
Sparrow	500
Shrew	600
Hummingbird (hovering)	1,200

Hummingbird

Hearing ranges of selected animals

Sound is measured by its pitch in units called Hertz (Hz). A higher number means a higher pitch – a lower number, a lower pitch.

Species	Hearing ranges in Hz
Elephant	1–20,000
Dog	10–35,000
Human	20–20,000
Bat	100–100,000
Frog	100–2,500

Hearing facts

- Crickets have "ears" on their knees made from a taut membrane that is sensitive to sound vibrations.
- Owls' left and right ears are often at different levels in the skull. This helps them to track their prey more effectively.

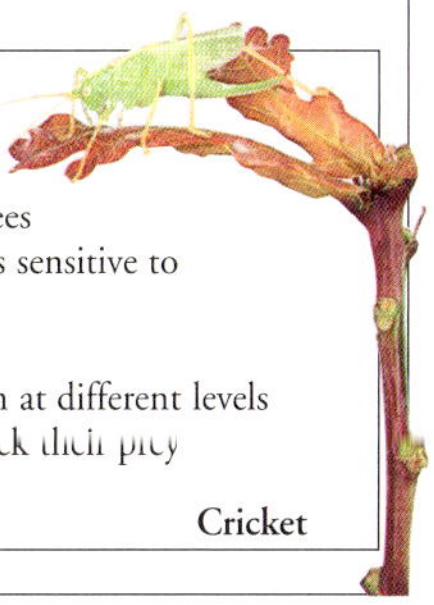

Cricket

Sleep requirements

This list excludes periods of hibernation, which can last up to several months.

Animal	Average hours of sleep per day
Koala	22
Sloth	20
Opossum	19
Cat	15
Squirrel	14

Domestic cat

Sleeping facts

- Big cats, such as leopards, sleep for about 12–14 hours a day. Since they have no natural enemies, they can sleep unprotected in the open air.
- Sloths are among the world's sleepiest animals. They hang upside down and sleep for up to 20 hours per day. Some species of sloth leave their trees only once a week.

PLANT AND ANIMAL RECORDS

THE PLANT AND ANIMAL kingdoms are the two largest groups of living things. These pages list the world's record breakers from the smallest and most poisonous frogs to the tallest and heaviest trees. Living things of the same species vary in size, so all measurements are approximate.

TREES

TALLEST SPECIES: Eucalyptus. These trees can grow to more than 130 m (427 ft) in height.

HEAVIEST SPECIES: Giant sequoia. Also known as wellingtonias, these conifers weigh up to 2,000 tonnes (tons).

OLDEST SPECIES: Ginkgo. This ancient species first appeared about 160 million years ago in China.

Coast redwood

Bristlecone pine

OLDEST LIVING TREE: Bristlecone pine. Native to Arizona and Nevada, USA, this species can live for more than 5,000 years.

MOST DROUGHT-RESISTANT TREE: Baobab. This African tree can store up to 136,000 litres (29,920 UK gallons) of water in its trunk.

WORLD'S TALLEST LIVING TREE: A coast redwood in Montgomery State Reserve, California, USA. It stands 112.01 m (368 ft) tall.

WORLD'S BIGGEST LIVING TREE: The General Sherman giant sequoia in Sequoia National Park, California, USA. It is 84 m (276 ft) tall and its base is approximately 10 m (33 ft) wide.

FUNGI

Fungi used to be classified as plants, but, since 1969, botanists have classified them as a separate kingdom.

BIGGEST FUNGUS: Bracket fungus. This huge species measures several metres across.

MOST POISONOUS FUNGUS: Death cap. If eaten, this deadly mushroom can cause death within 15 hours.

Death cap mushrooms

FLOWERING PLANTS

LARGEST FLOWER: Giant rafflesia. This foul-smelling flower can grow up to 1.05 m (3.5 ft) across and weigh as much as 7 kg (15.4 lb).

SMALLEST FLOWER: Australian duckweed. The flowers of this floating plant measure only 0.61 mm (0.024 in) across.

SMALLEST LAND PLANT: Dwarf snow willow. This miniscule plant grows only a few centimetres long.

LONGEST SEAWEED: Pacific giant kelp seaweed. The fronds of this seaweed can grow as long as 60 m (197 ft).

FASTEST-GROWING PLANT: Bamboo. This is the tallest and fastest-growing grass. Some species can grow to 30 m (98.4 ft) at a rate of 1 m (3.2 ft) a day.

Dioon edule. This evergreen shrub grows at a rate of only 0.76 mm (0.29 in) per year.

Bamboo

Snow willow

LEAVES

LARGEST LEAF: Raffia palm. Its leaves grow up to 20 m (66 ft) long.

SMALLEST LEAF: Floating duckweed. The leaves of this tiny plant are only 0.6 mm (0.02 in) long and 0.3 mm (0.01 in) wide.

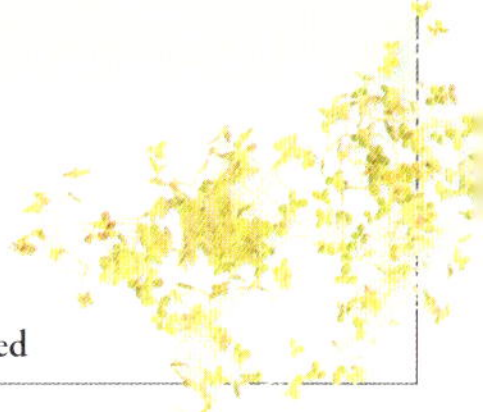

Duckweed

SEEDS

LARGEST SEED: Coco-de-mer palm. Each seed can weigh up to 20 kg (44 lb) and take ten years to develop.

SMALLEST SEED: A species of orchid. A billion seeds weigh as little as 1 g (0.035 oz).

Coco-de-mer seed

Orchids

MOST POISONOUS ANIMALS

REPTILE: *Hydrophis belcheri*. This sea snake is far more poisonous than any land snake. The Australian taipan is the deadliest land snake. Its bite is fatal without an antitoxin that counteracts the venom.

FISH: Death puffer. This harmless looking fish keeps poison in its blood and organs. If eaten, it can kill a person.

ARACHNID: Brazilian wandering spider. This aggressive spider bites if disturbed.

MOLLUSC: Blue-ringed octopus. The painful bite of this Australian octopus can kill in minutes.

AMPHIBIAN: Golden-yellow poison-dart frog. The colourful poison-dart frogs from South and Central America and the Madagascan mantellas have highly poisonous chemicals in their skins.

Golden mantella

Mammals

Largest mammal: Blue whale. The world's heaviest and longest animal, it can grow up to 35 m (115 ft) long and weigh up to 190 tonnes (tons).

Largest land mammal: African elephant. The average male elephant is 3 m (9.8 ft) tall and weighs about 5 tonnes (tons).

Tallest mammal: Giraffe. The adult male giraffe can grow up to 5.9 m (19.4 ft) tall.

Smallest mammal: Kitti's hog-nosed bat. Sometimes known as bumblebee bats, these tiny creatures have an average length of 3.3 cm (1.3 in) and weigh no more than 2 g (0.07 oz).

Smallest land mammal: African pygmy shrew. From head to tail, it is only 70 mm (2.7 in) long and weighs between 1.5–2.5 g (0.05–0.08 oz).

Heaviest primate: Gorilla. The male gorilla can weigh as much as 220 kg (485 lb).

Largest flying mammal: A flying fox (fruit bat of tropical Africa and Asia) can grow to the size of a small dog and have a wingspan of 2 m (6 ft).

Blue whale

Reptiles and amphibians

Largest lizard: Komodo dragon lizard. This Indonesian reptile grows up to 3 m (10 ft) long and weighs up to 166 kg (365 lb).

Smallest lizard: British Virgin Island gecko. This tiny lizard is only 18 mm (0.7 in) long.

Longest reptile: Saltwater crocodile. This is the longest animal on land, growing up to 6 m (20 ft) long.

Largest amphibian: Giant salamander. The average length of the Chinese giant salamander is 1.5 m (5 ft).

Smallest amphibian: Sminthillus limbatus. This tiny frog from Cuba is only 1 cm (0.5 in) long.

Largest turtle: Leatherback turtle. This turtle can grow more than 2 m (6.6 ft) long and weigh up to 450 kg (1,000 lb).

Saltwater crocodile

Snakes

Anaconda

Longest snake: Anaconda. The average length of the South American anaconda is 5.5 m (18 ft).

Shortest snake: Thread snake. This tiny snake from the West Indies is less than 11 cm (4.4 in) long.

Longest fangs: Gaboon viper. Its fangs can be as long as 5 cm (2 in).

Fastest snake: Black mamba. This African snake can travel at speeds of up to 19 kmh (12 mph).

Spiders and insects

Goliath beetle

Largest spider: Goliath bird-eating spider. The largest specimen on record had a legspan of 28 cm (11 in).

Largest web: Orb-web spider. Tropical orb-web spiders can spin webs of up to 1.5 m (5 ft) in circumference.

Largest butterfly: Queen Alexandra's birdwing. It is the largest and heaviest butterfly with a wingspan of up to 28 cm (11 in).

Largest prehistoric insect: Dragonfly. This huge insect had a wingspan of 75 cm (29.5 in).

Longest insect: Giant stick insect. This insect from New Guinea has an average length of 45 cm (17.7 in).

Largest wingspan: Owlet moth. Its wingspan can measure up to 30 cm (12 in).

Heaviest insect: Goliath beetle. This huge African beetle weighs up to 100 g (3.5 oz).

Smallest insect: Fairyfly wasp. These tiny wasps grow only 0.2 mm (0.007 in) long.

Fairyfly wasp

Marine animals

Largest fish: Whale shark. Found in the Atlantic, Pacific, and Indian oceans, these huge fish can grow up to 12.65 m (41.5 ft) long.

Smallest fish: Dwarf goby. The average length of a male fish is only 6 mm (0.3 in).

Largest mollusc: Giant Atlantic squid. The largest specimens grow up to 17 m (55.7 ft) long.

Whale shark

Largest bivalve mollusc: Giant clam. It can weigh as much as 300 kg (661 lb) and grow to 1.15 m (3.7 ft).

Largest crustacean: Japanese spider crab. This huge crab has a legspan of 4 m (13 ft) and can weigh as much as 18.6 kg (41 lb).

Smallest crustacean: Alonella water flea. This tiny crustacean grows only 0.25 mm (0.1 in) long.

Birds

Largest flying bird: Great bustard. A male bird can weigh up to 19 kg (42 lb).

Largest flightless bird: Ostrich. The African ostrich weighs 130 kg (280 lb) and grows to a height of 2.7 m (8.9 ft).

Largest prehistoric bird: Elephant bird. This massive flightless bird from Madagascar weighed around 438 kg (966 lb) and stood 3 m (10 ft) tall.

Smallest bird: Bee hummingbird. This Cuban bird measures only 5.7 cm (2.2 in) and weighs just 1.6 g (0.05 oz).

Farthest migration: Arctic tern. Every year, this bird flies from the Arctic to the Antarctic and back again – a round trip of about 40,000 km (25,000 miles).

Albatross

Largest wingspan: Wandering albatross. The wingspan of this huge seabird can stretch up to 3.6 m (12 ft) across.

Largest egg: Ostrich egg. The largest specimens can weigh up to 1.65 kg (3.64 lb) and measure up to 20 cm (8 in) long.

Smallest egg: Bee hummingbird egg. These eggs weigh only 0.25 g (0.009 oz).

Ostrich egg

WILDLIFE IN DANGER

Atlantic Empress disaster, 1979

SINCE LIFE BEGAN on Earth, many species of plants and animals have died out – mostly because of human interference. The main threats to wildlife today are habitat destruction, hunting and collecting, and pollution. Many plants and animals are now protected by law.

ENVIRONMENTAL DISASTERS

In 1989, the *Exxon Valdez* oil tanker ran aground in Alaska. It spilled more than 35,000 tonnes of oil into the Pacific, causing the deaths of thousands of seabirds. The table below lists the world's worst oil spills.

TANKER (LOCATION OF DISASTER)	DATE	OIL SPILLAGE IN TONNES
Atlantic Empress and *Aegean Captain* (Trinidad)	July 1979	300,000
Castillio de Bellver (Cape Town, South Africa)	August 1983	255,000
Olympic Bravery (Ushant, France)	January 1976	250,000
Showa-Maru (Malacca, Malaysia)	June 1975	237,000
Amoco Cadiz (Finistère, France)	March 1978	223,000
Odyssey (Atlantic Ocean, Canada)	November 1988	140,000
Torrey Canyon (Scilly Isles, UK)	March 1967	120,000
Sea Star (Gulf of Oman)	December 1972	115,000
Irenes Serenada (Pílos, Greece)	February 1980	102,000
Urquiola (Corunna, Spain)	May 1976	101,000

ENVIRONMENT FACTS

- It is estimated that over the next 20 years almost half a million species of plants and animals will become extinct.
- The ivory-billed woodpecker used to live in forest swamps. It is one of the world's rarest birds and is endangered.
- All species of rhinoceros are now protected by law. Many rhinoceroses were killed for their horns, which are reputed to have medicinal qualities.
- The population of the Komodo dragon, the largest-living lizard, is at a dangerously low level because of over-hunting by collectors.
- Turtles are often hunted for their shell, eggs, and meat. Several species of marine turtles are under threat.

Green turtle

ENDANGERED PLANTS

Habitat destruction, wetland drainage, urban growth, and modern farming methods threaten many plant species. Those most at risk are listed below.

COMMON NAME (LOCATION)	SCIENTIFIC NAME
Wild sago (USA)	Zania floridans
Chiapas slipper orchid (Mexico)	Phragmipedium exstaminodium
Sea bindweed (Europe)	Calystegia soldanella
Green pitcher plant (USA)	Sarracenia oreophila
Big-leaf palm (Madagascar)	Marojejya darianii
Socotran pomegranate (Yemen)	Punica protopunica
African violet (East Africa)	Saintpaulia ionantha
Green daffodil (Mediterranean)	Narcissus viridiflorus
Blue vanda (India/Thailand)	Vanda coerulea
Drago, or Canadian dragon, tree (Canary Islands/Madeira)	Dracaena draco
Caoba (Ecuador)	Persea theobromifolia

Sea bindweed

ENDANGERED ANIMALS

Endangered species all around the world are monitored by animal welfare organizations. The animals below are at risk of becoming extinct in the near future.

COMMON NAME (LOCATION)	SCIENTIFIC NAME
Blue whale (Antarctic Ocean)	*Balaenoptera musculus*
Black-footed ferret (North America)	*Mustela nigripes*
Giant panda (China)	*Ailuropoda melanoleuca*
Kemp's Ridley sea turtle (Mexico)	*Lepidochelys kempii*
Javan rhinoceros (Southeast Asia)	*Rhinoceros sondaicus*
Woolly spider monkey (Brazil)	*Bracyteles arachnoides*
Queen Alexandra's birdwing butterfly (Papua New Guinea)	*Ornithoptera alexandrae*
Mediterranean monk seal (Mediterranean coasts)	*Monachus monachus*
Yangtze river dolphin (China)	*Lipotes vexillifer*
Magpie robin (Seychelles)	*Copsychus sechellarun*
Californian condor (California, USA)	*Gymnogyps californianus*
Florida manatee (Atlantic Ocean)	*Trichechus manatus*

Blue whale

DWINDLING FORESTS

Humans have destroyed almost half of the world's tropical rainforests. This table shows how many forests are being cut down annually for timber or building projects.

COUNTRY	ANNUAL LOSS IN KM2 (MILES2)
Brazil	17,658 (6,818)
Venezuela	9,240 (3,568)
Indonesia	8,440 (3,259)
Zaire	7,344 (2,836)
Bolivia	5,916 (2,284)
Mexico	5,161 (1,993)
Colombia	3,717 (1,435)
Peru	2,968 (1,146)
Burma	2,392 (924)
Malaysia	1,860 (718)

South American rainforest

ENVIRONMENTAL ORGANIZATIONS

These environmental organizations are dedicated to helping plants and animals in danger and finding solutions to worldwide ecological problems.

GREENPEACE
Greenpeace
Canonbury Villas
London N1 2PN
www.greenpeace.org

FRIENDS of the earth
Friends of the Earth
26–28 Underwood Street
London N1 7JQ
www.foei.org

IFAW
International Fund for Animal Welfare
87-90 Albert Embankment
London SE1 7UD
www.ifaw.org

WWF
World Wildlife Fund
Panda House
Weyside Park
Godalming
Surrey GU7 1XR
www.wwf.org

UNIVERSE

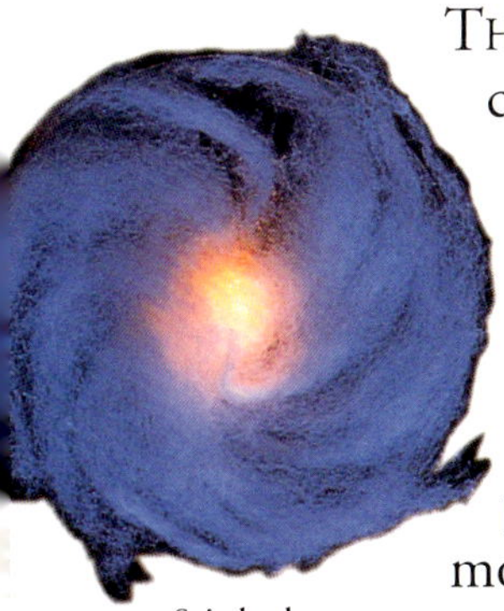

Spiral galaxy

THE KNOWN UNIVERSE contains countless millions of galaxies and stars. From Earth, the stars seem to form patterns in the sky. These patterns are known as constellations. We see different star patterns from month to month as Earth orbits the Sun.

SUN DATA

- Age: About 5 billion years
- Diameter: 1,392,000 km (865,000 miles)
- Distance from the Earth: 149.6 million km (92.9 million miles)
- Time taken to orbit galaxy: 240 million years
- Surface temperature: 5,500°C (9,900°F)
- Life expectancy: 10 billion years
- Mass (Earth = 1): 332,946

MOON DATA

- Age: 4.6 billion years
- Diameter: 3,476 km (2,160 miles)
- Distance from the Earth: 384,000 km (238,000 miles)
- Surface temperature: –173 to 105°C (–279 to 221°F)
- Mass (Earth = 1): 0.012
- Gravity (Earth = 1): 0.16
- Rotation period: 27.3 days
- The pull of the Moon's gravity is largely responsible for the rise and fall of tides on Earth.

CONSTELLATIONS OF THE NORTHERN HEMISPHERE

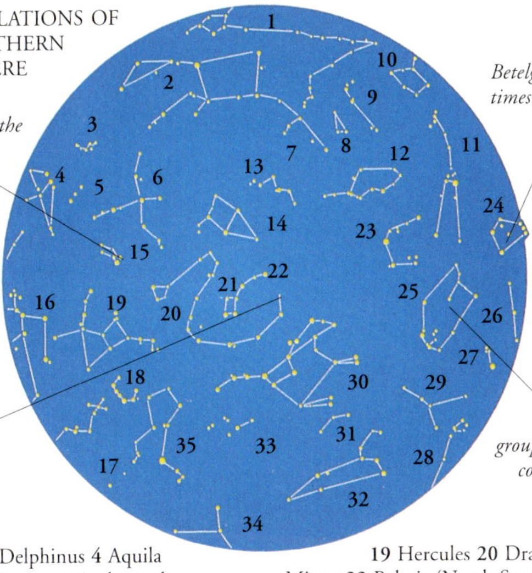

1 Pisces
2 Pegasus 3 Delphinus 4 Aquila
5 Sagitta 6 Cygnus 7 Andromeda
8 Triangulum 9 Aries 10 Cetus
11 Taurus 12 Perseus 13 Cassiopeia
14 Cepheus 15 Lyra 16 Ophiuchus
17 Serpens Caput 18 Corona Borealis
19 Hercules 20 Draco 21 Ursa Minor 22 Polaris (North Star) 23 Auriga
24 Orion 25 Gemini 26 Monoceros
27 Canis Minor 28 Hydra 29 Cancer
30 Ursa Major 31 Leo Minor 32 Leo
33 Canes Venatici 34 Virgo 35 Boötes

CONSTELLATIONS OF THE SOUTHERN HEMISPHERE

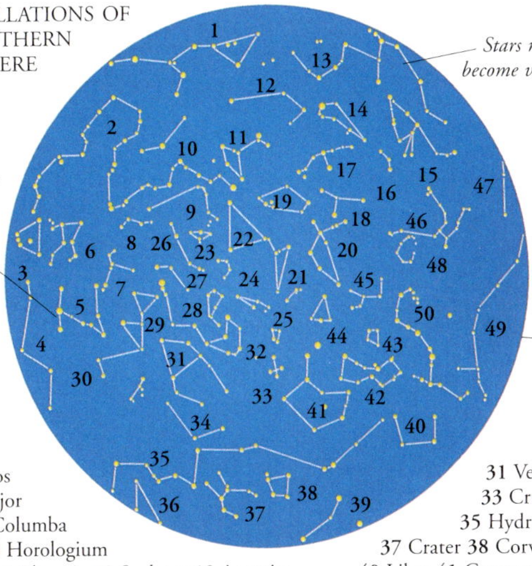

1 Cetus
2 Eridanus
3 Orion
4 Monoceros
5 Canis Major
6 Lepus 7 Columba
8 Caelum 9 Horologium
10 Fornax 11 Phoenix 12 Sculptor 13 Aquarius
14 Piscis Austrinus 15 Capricornus
16 Microscorpium 17 Grus 18 Indus 19 Tucana
20 Pavo 21 Apus 22 Hydrus 23 Reticulum
24 Mensa 25 Chameleon 26 Dorado 27 Pictor
28 Volans
29 Carinar
30 Puppis
31 Vela 32 Musca
33 Crux 34 Antlia
35 Hydra 36 Sextans
37 Crater 38 Corvus 39 Virgo
40 Libra 41 Centaurus 42 Lupus
43 Norma 44 Triangulum Australe
45 Ara 46 Sagittarius 47 Aquila
48 Corona Australis
49 Ophiuchus 50 Scorpius

INNER PLANETS / OUTER PLANETS

PLANETS	MERCURY	VENUS	EARTH	MARS	JUPITER	SATURN	URANUS	NEPTUNE	PLUTO
The nine planets in our solar system divide into two groups: the dense, rocky inner planets and the gaseous, icy outer planets.									
DISTANCE FROM THE SUN IN MILLIONS OF KM (MILES)	57.9 (36)	108.2 (67.2)	149.6 (93)	227.9 (141.6)	778.3 (483.6)	1,427 (886.7)	2,871 (1,784)	4,497 (2,794)	5,914 (3,675)
DIAMETER IN KM (MILES)	4,878 (3,031)	12,103 (7,520)	12,756 (7,926)	6,786 (4,217)	142,984 (88,850)	120,536 (74,901)	51,118 (31,764)	49,528 (30,775)	2,284 (1,419)
TIME TAKEN TO ORBIT THE SUN	87.97 days	224.7 days	365.26 days	686.98 days	11.86 years	29.46 years	84.01 years	164.79 years	248.54 years
TIME TAKEN TO TURN ON AXIS	58 days, 16 hours	243 days, 14 hours	23 hours, 56 mins	24 hours, 37 mins	9 hours, 55 mins	10 hours, 40 mins	17 hours, 14 mins	16 hours, 7 mins	6 days, 9 hours
SURFACE TEMPERATURE	–180 to 430°C (–292 to 806°F)	500°C (900°F)	–70 to 55°C (–94 to 131°F)	–120 to 25°C (–184 to 77°F) At cloud tops	–150°C (–238°F) At cloud tops	–180°C (–292°F) At cloud tops	–210°C (–346°F) At cloud tops	–210°C (–346°F)	–220°C (–364°F)
NUMBER OF MOONS	0	0	1	2	61	31	27	13	1
MASS (EARTH = 1)	0.055	0.81	1	0.107	318	95.18	14.5	17.14	0.0022
DENSITY (WATER = 1)	5.43	5.25	5.52	3.95	1.33	0.69	1.29	2.1	2.03

EARTH

MORE THAN SEVENTY per cent of the Earth's surface is covered by water. Above sea level, Earth's land surface is made up of seven vast land masses called continents. The Earth is in a constant state of change, both above and below the surface. Most volcanoes and earthquakes are caused by the movements of huge rocky plates in the Earth's crust.

HIGHEST AND LOWEST POINTS IN THE WORLD

CONTINENT	HIGHEST POINT ABOVE SEA LEVEL	HEIGHT IN METRES (FEET)	LOWEST POINT BELOW SEA LEVEL	DEPTH IN METRES (FEET)
Asia	Mt. Everest	8,848 (29,030)	Dead Sea	–400 (–1,312)
Africa	Kilimanjaro	5,895 (19,341)	Qattâra Depression	–133 (–436)
North America	Denali (Mt. McKinley)	6,194 (20,323)	Death Valley	–86 (–282)
South America	Aconcagua	6,960 (22,834)	Peninsular Valdez	–40 (–131)
Antarctica	Vinson Massif	5,140 (16,864)	Bentley Subglacial Trench	–2,538 (–8,327)
Europe	Elbrus	5,633 (18,481)	Caspian Sea	–28 (–92)
Australia	Mt. Kosciusko	2,228 (7,310)	Lake Eyre	–16 (–52)

Highest mountains
The ten highest mountains in the world are all in the Himalayas, which lie between Tibet, China, and the Indian subcontinent.

DESERTS

LARGEST DESERTS	AREA IN KM²	AREA IN MILES²
Sahara (Africa)	9,065,000	3,500,000
Arabian (Asia)	1,300,000	502,000
Gobi (Asia)	1,040,000	402,000
Kalahari (Africa)	580,000	224,000
Great Sandy (Australia)	414,000	160,000
Chihuahua (USA)	370,000	143,000
Takla Makan (Asia)	320,000	198,848
Kara Kum (Asia)	310,000	120,000
Namib (Africa)	310,000	120,000
Thar (Asia)	260,000	100,000

Sahara Desert

OCEANS AND SEAS

The table below lists the world's largest oceans and seas.

NAME	AREA IN KM²	AREA IN MILES²
Pacific Ocean	165,241,000	63,800,000
Atlantic Ocean	81,500,000	31,500,000
Indian Ocean	73,452,000	28,360,000
Arctic Ocean	14,089,600	5,440,000
Arabian Sea	3,864,000	1,492,000
South China Sea	3,447,000	1,331,000
Caribbean Sea	2,753,000	1,063,000
Mediterranean Sea	2,505,000	967,000
Bering Sea	2,269,000	876,000

LARGEST LAKES AND INLAND SEAS

LAKE	LOCATION	AREA IN KM²	AREA IN MILES²
Caspian Sea	Asia	370,980	143,236
Lake Superior	Canada/USA	82,098	31,698
Lake Victoria	Africa	68,880	26,595
Lake Huron	Canada/USA	59,566	22,999
Lake Michigan	USA	57,754	22,999
Lake Tanganyika	Africa	32,891	12,699
Lake Baikal	Siberia	31,498	12,161
Aral Sea	Asia	31,080	12,000

Caspian Sea

LONGEST RIVERS

NAME (LOCATION)	LENGTH IN KM (MILES)
Nile (Africa)	6,695 (4,160)
Amazon (South America)	6,500 (4,040)
Yangtze (Asia)	6,300 (3,915)
Mississippi–Missouri–Red Rock (USA)	6,020 (3,741)
Yenisey–Angara–Selenga (Asia)	5,540 (3,442)

Greatest waterfalls
The world's highest waterfalls are the Angel Falls in Venezuela. They were discovered by US pilot James Angel in 1935.

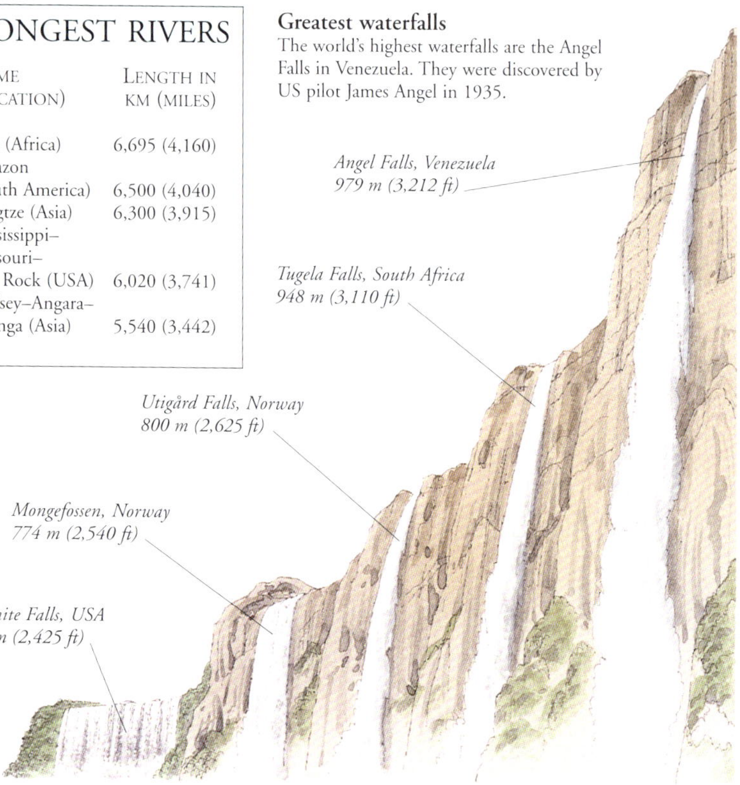

EARTH FACTS

- Diameter: 12,756 km (7,926 miles) at equator; 12,713 km (7,899 miles) at poles
- Age: 4.6 billion years old
- Distance from Sun: 150 million km (93 million miles)
- Mass: 5,854 billion billion tonnes
- Area: 29.2% land, 70.8% water
- Orbiting time: 365.26 days
- Orbiting speed: 29.8 km/sec (18.5 miles/sec)

Earthquakes

There are two different scales for measuring earthquakes: the Richter scale and the modified Mercalli scale.

Richter scale

The Richter scale was devised by American seismologist Charles F. Richter in 1935. It measures magnitude (the size of the shock wave and the energy it produces). Each number in the scale represents a shock ten times that of the previous one.

Early Chinese seismoscope

Modified Mercalli scale

The modified Mercalli scale measures how much an earthquake shakes the ground at a particular place. The original scale was devised by Italian Giuseppe Mercalli (1850–1914) in 1902. On Mercalli's scale, earthquakes are graded from one to ten.

Magnitude	Probable effects
1	Detectable by instruments.
2–2.5	Can be felt by people.
4–5	May cause slight damage.
6	Fairly destructive.
7	A major earthquake.
8–9	A very destructive earthquake.

Intensity	Probable effects
1	Not felt by people, but recorded by instruments.
2	Felt by people resting.
3	Detected indoors. Hanging objects swing.
4	Doors rattle. Trees shake.
5	Felt outdoors by most people. Objects move.
6	Felt by everyone. Windows break.
7	Difficult for people to stand. Bricks and tiles fall.
8	Major damage to buildings. Tree branches break.
9	Damage to foundations. Some buildings collapse.
10	Large landslides. Many buildings are destroyed.
11	Major ground disturbances. Railway lines buckle.
12	Total destruction. River courses altered.

Earthquake damage, San Francisco, USA, 1989

Earthquake facts

- The first instrument for recording earthquakes was the seismoscope, invented in China in AD 132.
- The worst earthquake in the 20th century was the Tangshan earthquake in China in 1976. It measured 7.8 on the Richter scale and approximately 242,000 people were killed.

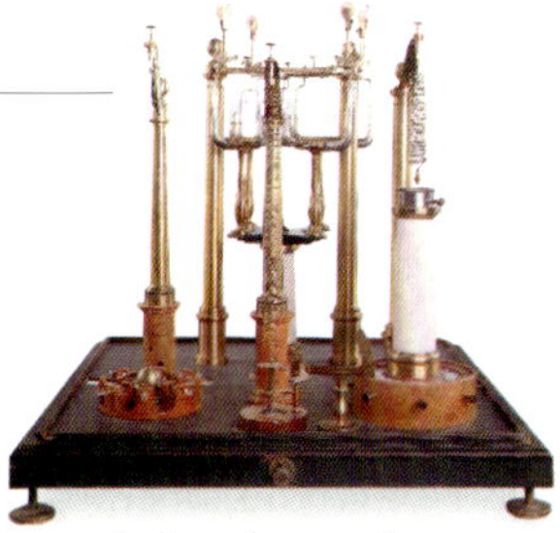

Italian seismograph

Extreme weather

Norilsk, Russia

LOWEST TEMPERATURE: –89.2°C (-128.6°F) at Vostok, Antarctica in 1983.

HIGHEST TEMPERATURE in shade: 57.7°C (136°F) at Al 'Aziziyah, Libya in 1922.

HIGHEST ANNUAL RAINFALL: 26,461 mm (1,041.7 in) during a 12-month period at Cherrapunji, India.

MOST RAINY DAYS: Mt. wai-ale-ale, Hawaii, which has on average 335 rainy days each year.

SUNNIEST PLACE: Yuma, Arizona, USA averages 4,127 hours of sunshine each year.

DRIEST PLACE: Atacama Desert, Chile has virtually no rain throughout the year.

HOTTEST PLACE: Dallol, Ethiopia has an average annual temperature of 34°C (90°F).

SNOWIEST PLACE: Mt. Rainier, USA, where 31,102 mm (1,224.5 in) of snow fell over a 12-month period in 1972–73.

Atacama Desert, Chile

COLDEST INHABITED PLACE: Norilsk, Russia has an average annual temperature of 10.9°C (12.4°F).

HIGHEST WIND SPEED: 372km/h (231mph) at Mt. Washington, USA on 12 April 1934.

WORST HAILSTORM: Moradabad, Uttar Pradesh, India, where 246 people were killed in 1888.

Beaufort scale

The Beaufort scale measures wind speed. It is used worldwide in weather reports and shipping forecasts. It was devised in 1805 by British Admiral Sir Francis Beaufort (1774–1857).

Force	Description	Average speed km/h	Average speed mph
0	Calm	1	1
1	Light air	3	2
2	Light breeze	9	5
3	Gentle breeze	15	10
4	Moderate breeze	25	15
5	Fresh breeze	35	21
6	Strong breeze	45	28
7	Moderate gale	56	35
8	Fresh gale	68	43
9	Strong gale	81	50
10	Whole gale	94	59
11	Storm	110	69
12	Hurricane	118	74

Volcanoes

Worst volcanic eruptions

Volcanic glass

Location	Date	Fatalities
Vesuvius, Italy	ad 79	20,000
Mt. Etna, Italy	1169	15,000
Vesuvius, Italy	1631	18,000
Mt. Etna, Italy	1669	20,000
Laki, Iceland	1783	20,000
Miyi-Yama, Java	1793	53,000
Tambora, Indonesia	1815	92,000
Krakatoa, Sumatra/Java	1883	36,380
Mont Pelée, Martinique	1902	40,000
Nevado del Ruiz, Colombia	1985	22,940

Major active volcanoes

Name	Height in metres (ft)	Last erupted
Mt. St Helens, USA	2,549 (8,362)	1998
Ruapehu, New Zealand	2,796 (9,173)	1999
Kliuchevskoi, Siberia	4,850 (15,912)	2001
Nyamuragira, D.R. Congo	3,053 (10,016)	2001
Tungurahua, Ecuador	5,023 (16,475)	2002
Fuego, Guatemala	3,763 (12,342)	2002
Semeru, Indonesia	3,676 (12,057)	2002
Nyiragongo, D.R. Congo	3,465 (11,365)	2002
Mt. Etna, Sicily, Italy	3,350 (10,991)	2002
Soufriere, Montserrat	915 (3,002)	2002

Mt. Ruapehu, New Zealand

PERIODIC TABLE

THE PERIODIC TABLE CLASSIFIES chemical elements according to their atomic number and chemical properties. This chart arranges elements into vertical columns, called groups, and horizontal columns, called periods. Elements with similar chemical properties lie in the same vertical group.

TYPES OF ELEMENT KEY

- Alkali metals
- Alkaline-earth metals
- Transition metals
- Lanthanides
- Actinides
- Poor metals
- Semimetals
- Non-metals
- Noble gases

Non-metals
Non-metals include elements that are gases at room temperature (20°C/68°F), such as hydrogen and oxygen. Solid non-metals, such as sulphur and phosphorus, usually break very easily and are poor conductors of heat and electricty.

Sulphur

Poor metals
The poor metals are aluminium, gallium, indium, thallium, tin, lead, bismuth, and polonium. They are softer and weaker than other metals and melt more easily.

Aluminium

Alkali and alkaline-earth metals
At the beginning of the periodic table are two groups of highly reactive metals: the alkali and the alkaline-earth metals. Alkali metals, such as potassium, caesium, and rubidium, all react violently with water.

Like all alkali metals, sodium is soft enough to cut with a knife.

Example element: 58 140 Ce Cerium

The atomic number is the number of protons in the nuclei of the element's atoms.

The atomic mass is the mass of one atom of the element compared to one-twelfth of the mass of an atom of the element carbon.

Chemical symbol Each atom has a chemical symbol. It is used for identification in chemical equations.

Name of element

There are two alternative number systems for grouping the elements: Group 1–18 and Group I–O.

1	2	3	4	5	6	7	8	
1 1.01 H Hydrogen								
3 6.94 Li Lithium	4 9.01 Be Beryllium							
11 22.99 Na Sodium	12 24.31 Mg Magnesium							
19 39.1 K Potassium	20 40.08 Ca Calcium	21 44.96 Sc Scandium	22 47.88 Ti Titanium	23 50.94 V Vanadium	24 51.1 Cr Chromium	25 54.94 Mn Manganese	26 55.85 Fe Iron	27 C Cob
37 85.47 Rb Rubidium	38 87.62 Sr Strontium	39 88.91 Y Yttrium	40 91.22 Zr Zirconium	41 92.91 Nb Niobium	42 95.94 Mo Molybdenum	43 98 Tc Technetium	44 101.07 Ru Ruthenium	45 R Rhod
55 132.91 Cs Caesium	56 137.33 Ba Barium	57 138.91 La Lanthanum	72 178.49 Hf Hafnium	73 180.95 Ta Tantalum	74 183.85 W Tungsten	75 186.21 Re Rhenium	76 190.2 Os Osmium	77 I Iridi
87 223 Fr Francium	88 226.03 Ra Radium	89 227.03 Ac Actinium	104 261 Rh Rutherfordium	105 263 Db Dubnium	106 266 Sg Seborgium	107 264 Bh Bohrium	108 267 Hs Hassium	109 M Meitn
GROUP I	GROUP II							

Lanthanides	58 140.12 Ce Cerium	59 140.91 Pr Praseodymium	60 144.24 Nd Neodymium	61 145 Pm Promethium	62 150.36 Sm Samarium	63 151.96 Eu Europium	64 G Gadoli
Actinides	90 232.04 Th Thorium	91 231.04 Pa Protactinium	92 238.03 U Uranium	93 237.05 Np Neptunium	94 244 Pu Plutonium	95 243 Am Americium	96 C Curi

BOILING/MELTING POINTS

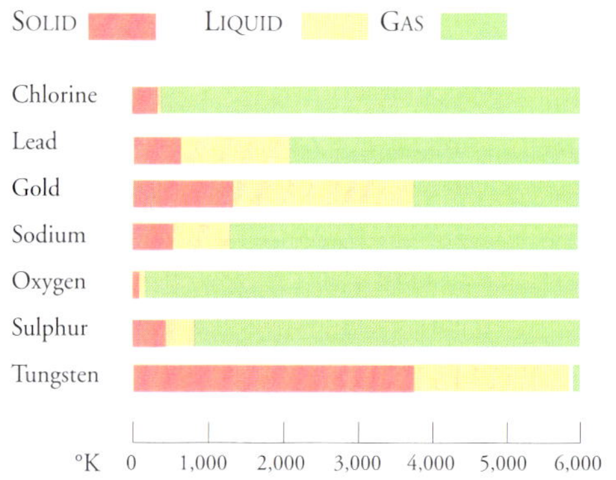

Copper
People have used copper to make weapons and tools for 8,000 years. It can be used on its own or mixed with other metals, such as tin or zinc, to form alloys.

Iodine
Iodine is a black solid that turns to gas very easily. Discovered in 1811, it used to be extracted from certain types of seaweed. Iodine compounds, called iodides, are used to make dyes.

NAMING ELEMENTS

he names of many elements are derived from Greek words. hey give clues about the elements' properties.

LEMENT/SYMBOL	GREEK WORD	MEANING
rgon (Ar)	*Argos*	Inactive
statine (At)	*Astatos*	Unstable
arium (Ba)	*Barys*	Heavy
romine (Br)	*Brómos*	Stench
hlorine (Cl)	*Chloros*	Pale green
ysprosium (Dy)	*Dusprositos*	Hard to get
ydrogen (H)	*Hydro genes*	Water forming
ercury (Hg)	*Hydrargyrum*	Liquid silver
hosphorus (P)	*Phosphoros*	Bringer of light
echnetium (Tc)	*Tekhnétos*	Artificial

Noble gases

The noble gases are helium, neon, argon, krypton, xenon, and radon. They form group 18 (O) of the periodic table and make up one per cent of the air. All noble gases have a full outer shell of electrons, which makes them extremely stable and unreactive.

Helium is the second lightest gas. It cannot catch fire, making it safe to use in balloons and airships.

Helium-filled balloons

ANCIENT ELEMENTS

ELEMENTS	KNOWN SINCE
Carbon	Prehistoric times
Sulphur	Prehistoric times
Gold	Prehistoric times
Lead	Prehistoric times
Copper	c.8000 BC
Silver	c.4000 BC
Iron	c.4000 BC
Tin	c.3500 BC
Mercury	c.1600 BC
Antimony	c.1000 BC

Halogens

The halogens are the gases and solid non-metals of group 17 (VII). They are all poisonous and have a strong smell.

Chlorine, a reactive green gas, is poisonous in large quantities.

Chlorine

nsition metals

transition metals form the central k of the periodic table. They ess reactive than the alkali alkaline-earth metals and higher melting and ing points.

is often used as a ective coating that ents iron or steel rusting.

0	11	12	13	14	15	16	17	18
								2 4 **He** Helium
			5 10.81 **B** Boron	6 12.01 **C** Carbon	7 14.01 **N** Nitrogen	8 16 **O** Oxygen	9 19 **F** Fluorine	10 20.18 **Ne** Neon
			13 26.98 **Al** Aluminium	14 28.09 **Si** Silicon	15 30.97 **P** Phosphorus	16 32.06 **S** Sulphur	17 35.45 **Cl** Chlorine	18 39.95 **Ar** Argon
58.69 **i** ckel	29 63.55 **Cu** Copper	30 65.39 **Zn** Zinc	31 69.72 **Ga** Gallium	32 72.59 **Ge** Germanium	33 74.92 **As** Arsenic	34 78.96 **Se** Selenium	35 79.9 **Br** Bromine	36 83.8 **Kr** Krypton
06.42 **d** dium	47 107.87 **Ag** Silver	48 112.41 **Cd** Cadmium	49 114.82 **In** Indium	50 118.71 **Sn** Tin	51 121.75 **Sb** Antimony	52 127.6 **Te** Tellurium	53 126.91 **I** Iodine	54 131.29 **Xe** Xenon
95.08 **t** inum	79 196.97 **Au** Gold	80 200.59 **Hg** Mercury	81 204.38 **Tl** Thallium	82 207.2 **Pb** Lead	83 208.98 **Bi** Bismuth	84 209 **Po** Polonium	85 210 **At** Astatine	86 222 **Rn** Radon
			GROUP III	GROUP IV	GROUP V	GROUP VI	GROUP VII	GROUP O

The Earth's crust

The bulk of the Earth's crust is oxygen and silicon, mostly combined in rocks or sand (silicon oxide). Clays are made of silicon and oxygen combined with aluminium, the third most common element.

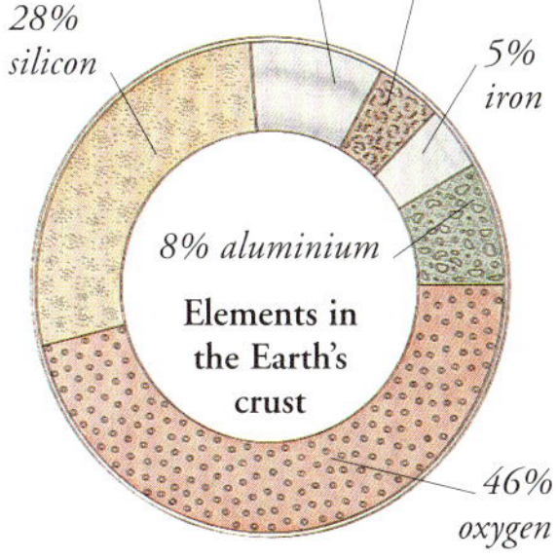

transition metals

ner transition series are the lanthanides and es. Uranium is a radioactive metal from the e series. Nuclear reactors use the isotope m–235 as a fuel.

Uranium fuel rod from a nuclear reactor

158.93 **b** bium	66 162.5 **Dy** Dysprosium	67 164.93 **Ho** Holmium	68 167.26 **Er** Erbium	69 168.93 **Tm** Thulium	70 173.04 **Yb** Ytterbium	71 174.97 **Lu** Lutetium
247 **k** elium	98 251 **Cf** Californium	99 252 **Es** Einsteinium	100 257 **Fm** Fermium	101 258 **Md** Mendelevium	102 259 **No** Nobelium	103 256 **Lr** Lawrencium

ELEMENTS PRODUCED ARTIFICIALLY

ELEMENT	YEAR PRODUCED	MAKER
Technetium	1937	C. Perrier & E. Segrè (Italy/USA)
Astatine	1940	D.R. Corson & others (USA)
Neptunium	1940	E.M. McMillan & P. Abelson (USA)
Plutonium	1940	G. Seaborg & others (USA)
Curium	1944	G. Seaborg & others (USA)
Americium	1945	G. Seaborg & others (USA)
Promethium	1945	J.A. Marinsky & others (USA)
Berkelium	1949	S.G. Thompson & others (USA)
Californium	1950	S.G. Thompson & others (USA)
Einsteinium	1952	A. Ghiorso & others (USA)
Fermium	1953	A. Ghiorso & others (USA)
Mendelevium	1958	A. Ghiorso & others (USA/USSR)
Nobelium	1958	A. Ghiorso & others (USA/USSR)
Lawrencium	1961	A. Ghiorso & others (USA/USSR)
Rutherfordium	1964	G. Flerov (USSR)
Dubnium	1968	A. Ghiorso (USA)
Seborgium	1974	A. Ghiorso (USA); G. Flerov (USSR)
Bohrium	1976	G. Munzenburg (Germany)
Meitnerium	1982	P. Armbruster (Germany)
Hassium	1984	P. Armbruster (Germany)

EMENT FACTS

statine is the rarest element on Earth. The rarest al is rhodium.

t room temperature, osmium is the densest nent, and lithium the least dense solid element.

• Hydrogen and helium are the most abundant elements in the universe.

• The tissues of the human body are made up of hydrogen, carbon, oxygen, and nitrogen, and bones contain calcium. Together, these five elements account for 98 per cent of the body's mass.

MATHEMATICS

MATHEMATICS IS THE study of number, shape, and quantity. Arithmetic is the basis of mathematics; it consists of addition, subtraction, division, and multiplication. Geometry is the study of lines, shapes, and angles.

Anatomy of a circle

A circle is a closed curve on which all points are equidistant from the centre. The diameter passes from one side to the other through the centre point. The ratio of the diameter to the circumference is expressed by pi π (approx. 3.141592).

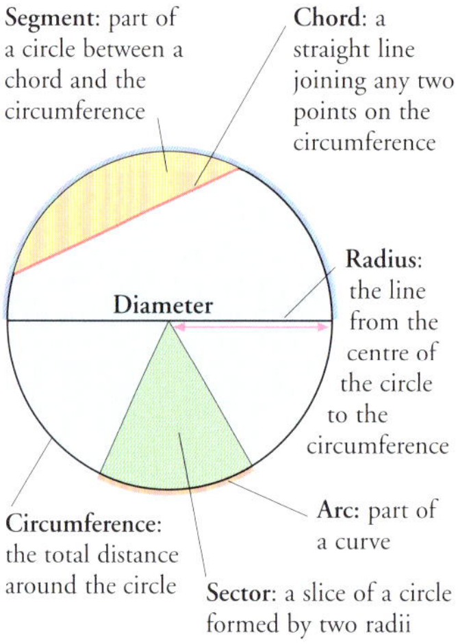

BINARY SYSTEM

The decimal number system is based on ten. From right to left, it increases in multiples of ten. The binary system is based on two. From right to left, it increases in multiples of two. Each digit is twice the value of the digit on its right.

BINARY				DECIMAL	
8	4	2	1	10	1
1	0	1	0	1	0
1	0	0	1		9
1	0	0	0		8
	1	1	1		7
	1	1	0		6
	1	0	1		5
	1	0	0		4
		1	1		3
		1	0		2
			1		1
			0		0

PRIME NUMBERS

A prime number can be divided only by itself and one. For example, 13 is a prime number. Nine is not a prime number; it can be divided by three, as well as by nine and one.

2	3	5	7
11	13	17	19
23	29	31	37
41	43	47	53
59	61	67	71
73	79	83	89
97	101	103	107
109	113	127	131

MATHEMATICAL SYMBOLS

SYMBOL	MEANING
+	Add (plus)
–	Subtract (minus)
x	Multiply (times)
÷	Divided by
=	Equal to
≠	Not equal to
>	Greater than
<	Less than
≥	Greater than or equal to
≤	Less than or equal to
∞	Infinity
%	Per cent
√	Square root of

PLANE AND SOLID SHAPES

Triangles

Triangles are three-sided plane figures with interior angles that combine to form 180°. The area of any triangle is: 1/2 x base x height.

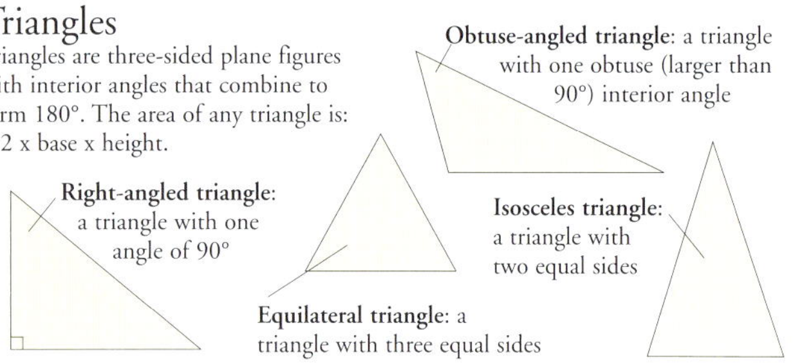

Plane figures

These are two-dimensional (flat) shapes.

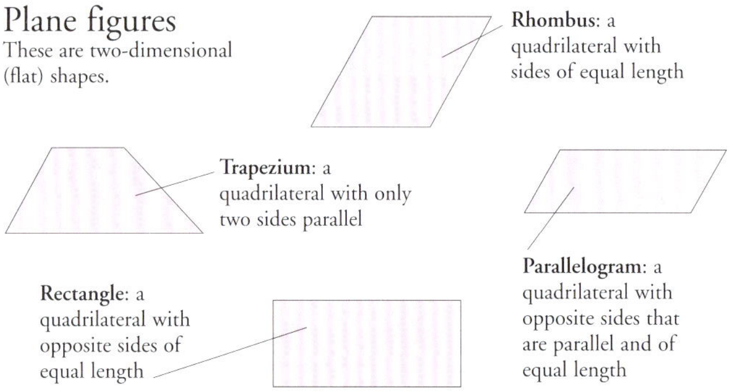

Solids

Solids are three-dimensional shapes. Polyhedrons are solids that have plane (flat) faces.

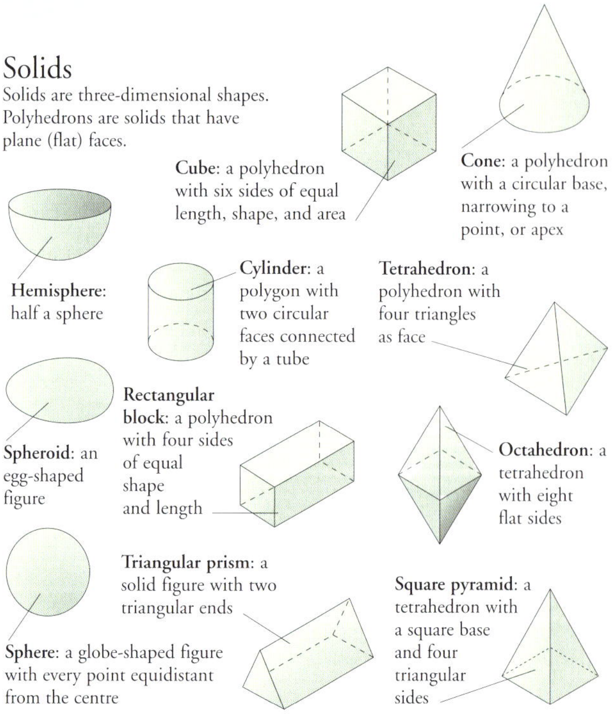

Polygons

A polygon is a plane figure with three or more straight sides.

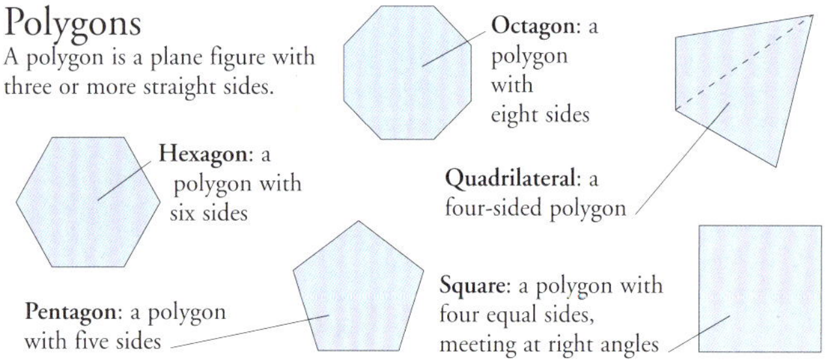

Angles and sides

NAME	NO. OF SIDES	INTERNAL ANGLES
Triangle	3	60°
Quadrilateral	4	90°
Pentagon	5	108°
Hexagon	6	120°
Heptagon	7	128.6°
Octagon	8	135°
Nonagon	9	140°
Decagon	10	144°
Undecagon	11	147.3°
Dodecagon	12	150°

WEIGHTS AND MEASURES

THERE ARE TWO major systems of measurement: metric and imperial. Although some countries, such as the United States, still use the older imperial system, scientists and most countries worldwide use metric.

THE SEVEN BASE SI UNITS

The main international system of standard units is called SI units. The seven "base units" are listed below. All other SI units are derived from them.

QUANTITY	UNIT	SYMBOL
Mass	Kilogram	kg
Length	Metre	m
Time	Second	s
Electric current	Ampere	A
Temperature	Kelvin	K
Luminous intensity	Candela	cd
Amount of substance	Mole	mol

NUMBER TERMS

PREFIX (SYMBOL)	EXAMPLE	MEANING
tera (T)	terametre	One million million
giga (G)	gigabyte	One thousand million
mega (M)	megawatt	One million
kilo (k)	kilogram	One thousand
hecto (h)	hectometre	One hundred
deci (d)	decimetre	One-tenth
centi (c)	centimetre	One-hundredth
milli (m)	millimetre	One-thousandth
micro (µ)	microsecond	One-millionth
nano (n)	nanosecond	One-thousand millionth

UNITS OF MEASUREMENT

Length

METRIC	
1 millimetre (mm)	
1 centimetre (cm)	= 10 mm
1 metre (m)	= 100 cm
1 kilometre (km)	= 1,000 m
IMPERIAL	
1 inch (in)	
1 foot (ft)	= 12 in
1 yard (yd)	= 3 ft
1 mile	= 1,760 yd

Spring balance

Area

METRIC	
1 square millimetre (mm^2)	
1 sq centimetre (cm^2)	= 100 mm^2
1 sq metre (m^2)	= 10,000 cm^2
1 hectare (ha)	= 10,000 m^2
1 sq kilometre (km^2)	= 1,000,000 m^2
IMPERIAL	
1 sq inch (in^2)	
1 sq foot (ft^2)	= 144 in^2
1 sq yard (yd^2)	= 9 ft^2
1 acre	= 4,840 yd^2
1 sq mile	= 640 acres

Mass and weight

METRIC	
1 gram (g)	
1 kilogram (kg)	= 1,000 g
1 tonne (t)	= 1,000 kg
IMPERIAL	
1 ounce (oz)	
1 pound (lb)	= 16 oz
1 stone	= 14 lb
1 hundredweight (cwt)	= 8 stones
1 ton	= 20 cwt

Ashanti gold weight

Volume

METRIC	
1 cubic millimetre (mm^3)	
1 cubic centimetre (cm^3)	= 1,000 mm^3
1 cubic metre (m^3)	= 1,000,000 cm^3
1 litre	= 1,000 cm^3
IMPERIAL	
1 cubic inch (in^3)	
1 cubic foot (ft^3)	= 1,728 in^3
1 cubic yard (yd^3)	= 27 ft^3
1 fluid ounce (fl oz)	
1 UK pint (pt)	= 20 fl oz
1 UK gallon (gal)	= 8 pt

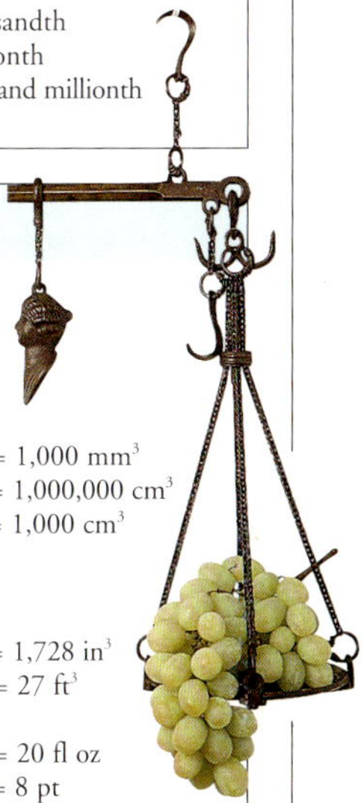

Roman weight

CONVERSION TABLES

Length conversion

TO CONVERT IMPERIAL:	INTO METRIC:	MULTIPLY BY:
Inches	Centimetres	2.54
Feet	Metres	0.3048
Yards	Metres	0.9144
Miles	Kilometres	1.6093

TO CONVERT METRIC:	INTO IMPERIAL:	MULTIPLY BY:
Centimetres	Inches	0.3937
Metres	Feet	3.2808
Metres	Yards	1.0936
Kilometres	Miles	0.6214
Metres	Furlongs	0.005
Metres	Fathoms	0.547
Kilometres	Nautical miles	0.54

Mass and weight conversion

TO CONVERT IMPERIAL:	INTO METRIC:	MULTIPLY BY:
Ounces	Grams	28.3495
Pounds	Kilograms	0.4536
Stones	Kilograms	6.3503
Hundredweights	Kilograms	50.802
Tons	Tonnes	1.0161

TO CONVERT METRIC:	INTO IMPERIAL:	MULTIPLY BY:
Grams	Ounces	0.0352
Kilograms	Pounds	2.2046
Kilograms	Stones	0.1575
Kilograms	Hundredweights	0.0197
Tonnes	Tons	0.9842

Yard stick

Area conversion

TO CONVERT IMPERIAL:	INTO METRIC:	MULTIPLY BY:
Sq inches	Sq centimetres	6.4516
Sq feet	Sq metres	0.0929
Sq yards	Sq metres	0.8361
Acres	Hectares	0.4047
Sq miles	Sq kilometres	2.59

TO CONVERT METRIC:	INTO IMPERIAL:	MULTIPLY BY:
Sq centimetres	Sq inches	0.155
Sq metres	Sq feet	10.7639
Sq metres	Sq yards	1.196
Hectares	Acres	2.4711
Sq kilometres	Sq miles	0.3861

Assyrian weight

Volume conversion

TO CONVERT IMPERIAL:	INTO METRIC:	MULTIPLY BY:
Cubic inches	Cubic cm (ml)	16.3871
Cubic feet	Litres	28.3169
Cubic yards	Cubic metres	0.7646
Fluid ounces	Cubic cm (ml)	28.413
UK pints	Litres	0.5683
UK gallons	Litres	0.4.546

TO CONVERT METRIC:	INTO IMPERIAL:	MULTIPLY BY:
Cubic centimetres (millilitres)	Cubic inches	0.061
	Fluid ounces	0.0352
Litres	Cubic feet	0.0353
Cubic metres	Cubic yards	1.308
Litres	UK pints	1.7598
Litres	UK gallons	0.22

Temperature conversions

- To convert °C to °F, multiply by 9, divide by 5, and add 32.
- To convert °F to °C, subtract 32, divide by 9, and multiply by 5.
- To convert °C to kelvin (K), add 273.15.
- To convert kelvin (K) to °C, subtract 273.15.

Celsius	Fahrenheit	Kelvin
100	212	373
90	194	363
80	176	353
70	158	343
60	140	333
50	122	323
40	104	313
30	86	303
20	68	293
10	50	283
0	32	273
-10	14	263
-20	-4	253

POLITICAL WORLD

THE WORLD IS DIVIDED into 193 independent countries. The line that separates one country from another is called a border. Disputed borders are marked on the map by a dotted line.

COUNTRY FACTS

- The world's largest country is the Russian Federation, with an area of 17,075,400 sq km (6,592,810 sq miles).
- The world's smallest country is the Vatican City, with an area of 0.44 sq km (0.17 sq miles).

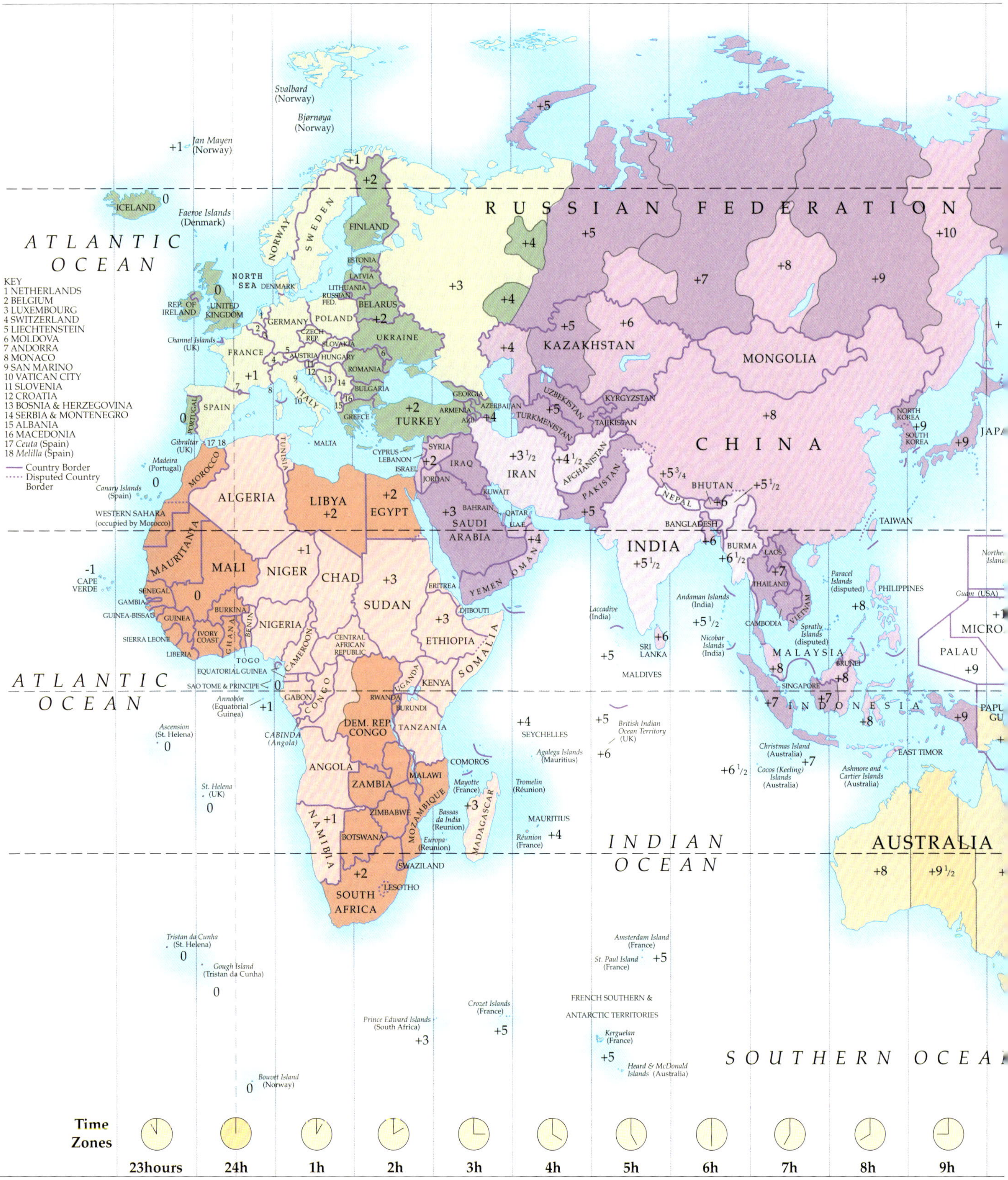

International time zones

The world is divided into 24 time zones, one for each hour of the day. Clocks in each zone are set to a different time. For instance, when it is noon in Greenwich, England, it is 10 p.m. in Sydney, Australia.

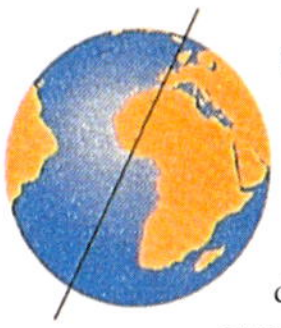

GMT

Greenwich Mean Time (GMT) refers to the exact time in Greenwich, England. In each time zone, clocks are set depending on whether they are east or west of Greenwich. The numbers on the map indicate the number of hours that must be added or subtracted to reach GMT.

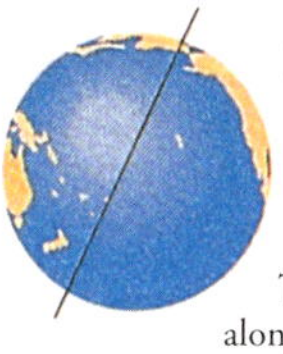

International Date Line

Lines of longitude and latitude are imaginary lines drawn on the Earth's surface. Meridians (lines of longitude) run from pole to pole. The International Date Line runs along the 180° meridian. When you cross this line from east to west, the date changes. The western side is a day ahead of the eastern side.

WORLD POPULATION

IN 1500, THE WORLD'S POPULATION was about 435 million. Today, it has grown to more than 6 billion, with a million children being born every day. The rapid growth in population since 1800 is largely due to improvements in food production and medical knowledge. In many parts of the world, rapid population growth causes serious problems, such as food shortages and overcrowding in cities.

URBAN POPULATION

In 1900, only 10 per cent of the world's population lived in cities. Today, that figure is about 50 per cent. This table lists the world's most populated urban areas (by administrative division).

URBAN AREA	POPULATION
Toyko	31,036,000
Mexico City	20,965,000
Seoul	19,844,000
New York	19,047,000
São Paulo	18,505,000
Jakarta	17,369,000
Dehli	16,713,000
Mumbai	16,687,000

Tokyo, Japan

World population
The map below shows population figures for the world's main land areas. Between them, China and India account for more than one third of the world's population.

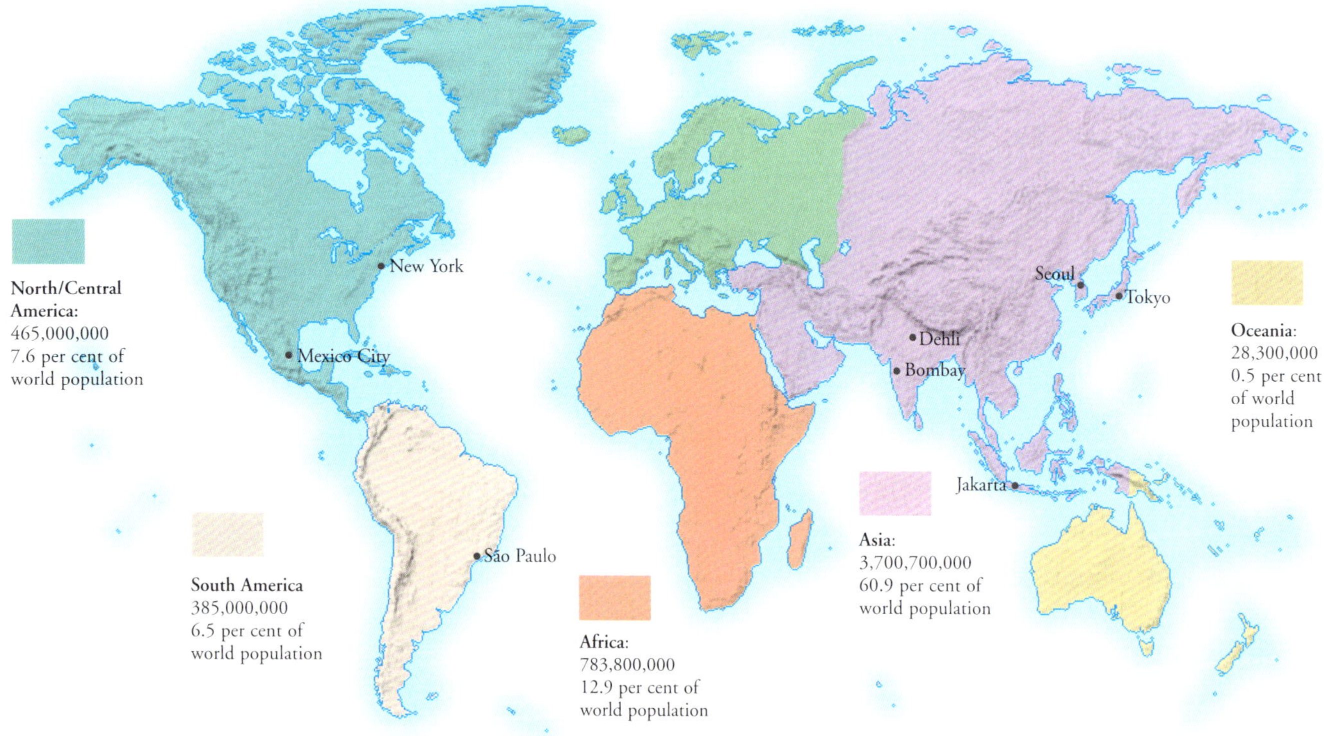

Europe: 704,900,000 11.6 per cent of world population

North/Central America: 465,000,000 7.6 per cent of world population

South America 385,000,000 6.5 per cent of world population

Africa: 783,800,000 12.9 per cent of world population

Asia: 3,700,700,000 60.9 per cent of world population

Oceania: 28,300,000 0.5 per cent of world population

Hutu refugees in Rwanda in 1996

REFUGEES

Throughout history, many millions of people have become refugees. Wars, drought, famine, and poverty are some of the reasons why people leave their homes and families. Today, almost 40 per cent of the world's refugees come from Asia.

World refugees (2002 figures)

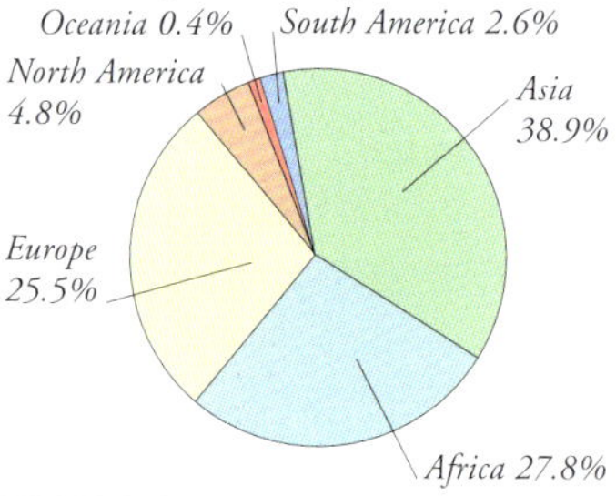

HIGHEST POPULATION

COUNTRY	POPULATION
China	1,290,000,000
India	1,030,000,000
USA	281,400,000
Indonesia	214,000,000
Brazil	172,600,000

LOWEST POPULATION

COUNTRY	POPULATION
Vatican	542
Tuvalu	11,300
Nauru	12,500
Palau	19,700
San Marino	26,900

FERTILITY RATES

Africa: 5.2
Asia: 2.7
S America: 2.6
Oceania: 2.4
N America: 2
Europe: 1.4

Figures shown are the average number of children per woman.

Fertility rates measure the average number of children born to each woman. Fertility rates are declining rapidly in the industrialized world, and are highest in Africa.

LIVING STANDARDS

Slovakian children

IN THE PAST 100 YEARS, living standards have improved greatly across the world. Better health care, even in poorer countries, means that fewer people now die of hunger and disease. Advances in medicine and improved diet and education have helped people to live longer and healthier lives. However, many problems remain, especially in the poorer countries of Africa and Asia.

LIFE EXPECTANCY

Life expectancy is the average length of time a person is likely to live. Wealthier countries generally have higher life expectancies than poorer countries. The world average life expectancy is 64.

Highest life expectancy (male)

COUNTRY	AGE
Japan	77.5
Singapore	77.1
Sweden	77
Australia	76.9
Switzerland	76.7

Highest life expectancy (female)

COUNTRY	AGE
Japan	84.1
Singapore	83.2
Canada	83
France	82.9
Australia	82.7

Japanese family

Lowest life expectancy (male)

COUNTRY	AGE
Zambia	37.1
Angola	37.1
Malawi	37.2
Botswana	38.6
Rwanda	38.6

Lowest life expectancy (female)

COUNTRY	AGE
Zimbabwe	36.3
Mozambique	36.7
Zambia	37.4
Malawi	38
Angola	39.6

PEOPLE PER DOCTOR

The table below compares the average number of people per doctor in some developed and developing countries.

COUNTRY	PEOPLE PER DOCTOR
Burkina	20,000
Ghana	16,700
Mali	10,000
Zimbabwe	10,000
Bangladesh	5,000
Thailand	2,500
Guatemala	1,111
USA	370
Austria	333
Georgia	263
Russian Federation	217

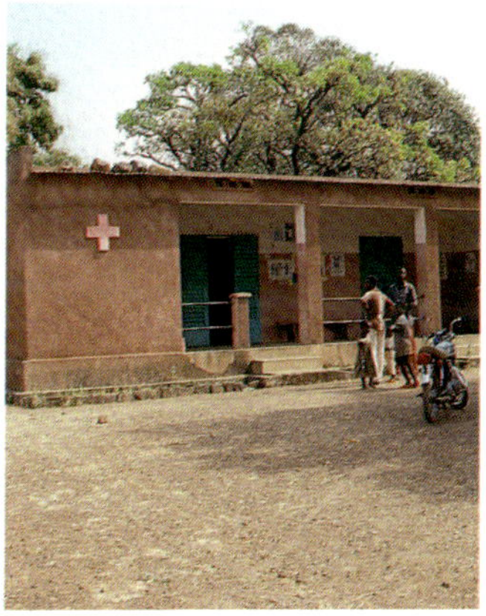

Rural hospital, Burkina

ADULT LITERACY

Adult literacy rates show how many adults over the age of 15 can read and write. The table below lists the average literacy rates for a variety of countries.

COUNTRY	PER CENT OF POPULATION
USA	99
UK	99
Brazil	85
China	84
Kuwait	83
India	57
Angola	40
Somalia	24
Niger	16

Shanty school in São Paulo, Brazil

SAFE WATER

Almost 2 billion people worldwide do not have access to the minimum level of safe water (20 litres/6 gallons per person per day). The table shows the average number of people with access to safe water in some developed and developing countries.

COUNTRY	PER CENT OF POPULATION
Tunisia	98
Saudi Arabia	93
Iran	90
Mexico	83
Zimbabwe	79
Pakistan	74
Kenya	53
Vietnam	43
Mali	37
Uganda	34
Ethiopia	26

Village well, Vietnam

MAJOR CAUSES OF DEATH

DEATH FACTS

- Worldwide, tuberculosis is the largest single cause of death. Two billion people are infected, just under a third of the total global population.
- Heart disease is the leading cause of death in Europe and North America, followed by depression-related illnesses.
- The UN estimates that more than 36 million people worldwide have HIV, with around 70 per cent of infections concentrated in sub-Saharan Africa.

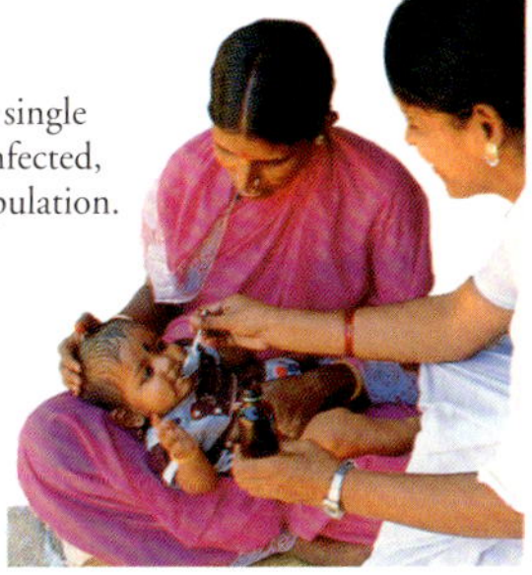

Nurse administering a vaccine

FOOD SUPPLY

The "Dietary Energy Supply" (DES) is the amount of calories available per person per day. The mimimum amount of calories needed per day is 2,300. This table compares the DES of various countries.

COUNTRY	CALORIES PER DAY
Denmark	3,780
Ireland	3,620
Japan	2,900
Uruguay	2,800
Chad	1,920
Somalia	1,580

WORLD RESOURCES

RAW MATERIALS ARE natural substances that are extracted from water, air, or from the ground. Some energy sources, such as solar or wind power, are renewable. Others, such as oil or coal, are non-renewable and will eventually run out. As world population grows, people are drawing more heavily on the Earth's natural resources.

LEADING AGRICULTURAL PRODUCERS

Today, farming is a major international business, with many countries competing in the export market. This table shows the top producers of a wide range of agricultural products.

PRODUCT	TOP PRODUCERS	PRODUCT	TOP PRODUCERS
Cattle	Australia	Rubber	Thailand
Cocoa	Ivory Coast	Sheep	Australia
Coffee	Brazil	Soya beans	USA
Cotton	China	Tea	India
Corn	USA	Tobacco	China
Cows' milk	India	Wheat	China
Hens' eggs	China	Wood	USA
Potatoes	Russian Federation	Wool	Australia

Tea

Coffee

Cotton

FOSSIL FUELS

Electricity

This table shows annual production in kilowatt hours.

COUNTRY	KW/HR
USA	3,600,000,000,000
China	1,200,000,000,000
Japan	1,000,000,000,000
Russia	798,000,000,000
Canada	567,000,000,000

Light bulb

Oil

This table shows oil production in tonnes per annum.

COUNTRY	TONNES
Saudi Arabia	441,200,000
USA	353,500,000
Russian Federation	323,300,000
Iran	186,600,000
Mexico	172,100,000

Oil plant, Libya

Coal

This table shows coal production in tonnes per annum.

COUNTRY	TONNES
USA	570,000,000
China	498,000,000
Australia	155,600,000
India	154,300,000
South Africa	118,800,000

Coal

Energy consumption

This table lists the major consumers of coal, oil, electricity, and gas.

COUNTRY	% OF WORLD TOTAL
USA	25%
China	10%
Russia	7%
Japan	5.8%
Germany	3.9%
India	3.1%
UK	2.6%

CROP PRODUCERS

Wheat

COUNTRY	TONNES PER ANNUM
China	94,181,100
India	68,458,000
USA	53,276,084
Russian Federation	46,871,000
France	32,065,000
Germany	22,888,608

Emmer

Rice

COUNTRY	TONNES PER ANNUM
China	181,514,992
India	131,900,000
Indonesia	49,400,000
Bangladesh	34,276,000
Vietnam	31,925,000
Thailand	25,200,000

Basmati rice

Maize (Corn)

COUNTRY	TONNES PER ANNUM
USA	239,521,424
China	110,390,000
Brazil	41,411,240
Mexico	18,615,904
France	16,478,000
Argentina	15,350,000

Maize (Corn)

MINERAL PRODUCERS

This table shows the world's major mineral producers.

MINERAL	TOP PRODUCERS	% OF WORLD TOTAL
Bauxite	Australia	30%
Copper	Chile	40%
Iron ore	China	20%
Salt	USA	22%
Uranium	USA	22%

WORLD CONSUMPTION

This table lists the nations with the highest rates of consumption per capita for a variety of commodities.

CEREALS	ROUNDWOOD
Morocco	Finland
Egypt	Guatemala
Algeria	Sweden
Syria	Canada
Turkey	Gabon
Burma	New Zealand

MEAT	PASSENGER CARS
USA	Italy
Cyprus	Germany
New Zealand	Australia
Australia	USA
Spain	Austria
Austria	Switzerland

FISH CATCHES

This table shows the biggest global fish catches per annum in tonnes.

COUNTRY	TONNES
China	39,300,000
Peru	8,437,000
Japan	5,935,000
Chile	5,325,000
India	5,244,000
USA	5,154,000
Indonesia	4,797,000
World total catch	**124,448,000**

Fishing in the USA